THE HOWLS
OF AUGUST

Encounters with Algonquin Wolves

To Dan Strickland and Ron Tozer —
mentors, tutors, and friends

For introducing me to the ways of the wolf and for
showing me by exemplary example how to interpret
the wonder of all living things to those less familiar
with the importance of it all.

THE HOWLS OF AUGUST

Encounters with Algonquin Wolves

Michael Runtz

The BOSTON
MILLS PRESS

Published in 1997 by
Boston Mills Press
132 Main Street
Erin, Ontario
N0B 1T0
www.boston-mills.on.ca

An affiliate of
Stoddart Publishing Co. Limited
34 Lesmill Road
Toronto, Ontario, Canada
M3B 2T6

Distributed in Canada by
General Distribution Services Inc.
30 Lesmill Road
Toronto, Canada M3B 2T6
Tel 416-445-3333
Fax 416-445-5967
e-mail customer.service@ccmailgw.genpub.com

Distributed in the United States by
General Distribution Services Inc.
85 River Rock Drive, Suite 202
Buffalo, New York 14207
Toll-free 1-800-805-1083
Fax 416-445-5967
e-mail customer.service@ccmailgw.genpub.com

01 00 99 98 97   2 3 4 5

Cataloging in Publication Data

Runtz, Michael W.P.
        The howls of August : encounters with Algonquin wolves

Includes bibliographical references.
ISBN 1-55046-195-8

1. Wolves - Ontario - Algonquin Provincial Park.   I. Title.

QL737.C22R86 1997   599.773'09713'147   97-931613-8

Design by Mary Firth
Copy-editing by Heather Lang-Runtz

Printed in Canada

CONTENTS

▼

ACKNOWLEDGMENTS

I must begin by thanking Dan Strickland and Ron Tozer for hiring me as a naturalist in Algonquin and introducing me to wolves way back when. Thanks also, for the "second chance."

I would also like to thank Ernie Martelle, former Superintendent of Algonquin Provincial Park, for granting me access to forest access roads in the park. As well, Doug Elliot, Nancy and Henry Checko, and other members of the Ministry of Natural Resources for notifying me of their wolf sightings. Thanks also to Ron Pittaway for providing the photo of Rosie and for the lessons on pishing and squeaking.

To Graham Forbes, Lee Swanson, and Carolyn Callaghan, wolf researchers extraordinaire, I remain indebted for your stimulating conservation, warm campfires, and various culinary delights (including those delicious peanut butter and honey sandwiches).

I would also like to thank A. Ron Wilson of Kodak Canada Inc. for supplying the fine film used in this book.

As always, a heartfelt thank you to my wife, Heather, and sons, Harrison and Dylan, for tolerating my frequent disappearances into wolf country.

And to the wolves of Algonquin, for providing so many unforgettable moments and for imparting some insight into the essence of life.

INTRODUCTION

While I have not yet danced with Algonquin Park wolves, for 25 years I have spent many memorable hours in close contact with these grand creatures. I have howled with them as a seasonal park naturalist, observed them as a natural history author, recorded them as a nature photographer, and appreciated them as a wilderness patron. The stories in this book recount some of my more intimate encounters with these remarkable animals.

Timber wolves figure prominently among the cast of Algonquin fauna. And although a number of supporting members, especially loons and moose, share the limelight, wolves continue to take top billing with the half-million visitors who come to Algonquin each year.

The only species to inspire such polar emotions, wolves are fiercely loved for their embodiment of wilderness, yet despised for their supposed irreverence for other creatures. They are indeed an enigma. Year after year thousands of admirers pour into Algonquin to savour a few seconds of their wild music, while just beyond the park's boundaries adversaries try to silence them forever.

Wolves are creatures of the night, and often only their tracks and scats document their comings and goings. Heard but seldom seen, they forcefully take from the wild what they need

 Timber wolves are one of Algonquin Park's main draws.

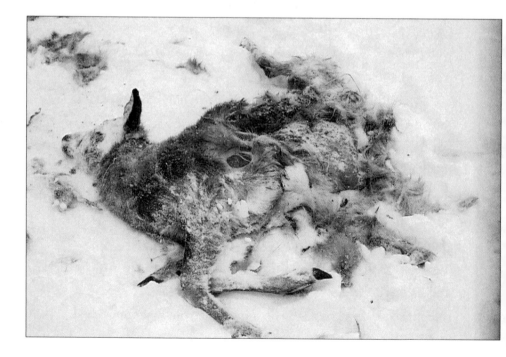

 The unpleasant sight of a wolf-killed animal is responsible for some of the ill feeling that prevails in my home region.

to survive. Is it not ironic that those characteristics that render wolves romantic to some elicit fear in others?

Competition for venison and moose meat is one possible reason for many hunters' contempt for wolves. But I believe an element of fear is also at work. Fear of the beast that kills without a gun. Fear of the shadow of death that lurks just beyond. And fear of one's own mortality if by chance we stumble across the messy remains of their victims. By killing the killer, perhaps an individual may be symbolically delaying his own inevitable fate.

Unlike most people, I have stared into the eyes of a wolf — and have never felt death's chill, merely a calm indifference. I have learned first-hand that wolves deserve only our respect, never our fear.

Although this book offers some insight into the life of the wolf, it is not a biological overview. Rather, it is a chronicle of my experiences with these animals over a quarter of a century. I have limited my stories to the seasonal period favoured by most of Algonquin's visitors, which happens to be when one is most likely to meet a wolf. Please join me as I relive my encounters with Algonquin wolves, the enduring spirit of this great park.

My first encounters with Algonquin wildlife were with deer, not wolves (PHOTO: JUNE RUNTZ).

C h a p t e r   1

FIRST ENCOUNTERS

nscribed on Tom Thomson's cairn at Canoe Lake in Algonquin Park are the words: "He lived humbly but passionately with the wild. It made him brother to all untamed things of nature. It drew him apart and revealed itself wonderfully to him." I have always loved this eloquent epitaph, partly because I can relate to Thomson's relationship with the wild. Since I was a young boy, I have been drawn to the natural world. Whenever I encounter a wild creature, whether a timber wolf in Algonquin Park or a crab spider in my backyard, I feel a kind of connection with it. I enter and leave its world feeling more like a part of it than an intruder.

I can trace this strong connection with nature to my earliest years, when my parents brought me to Algonquin Park to see white-tailed deer. But the clinching moment came when I was five years old. The woman who lived next door decided that bird-watching might keep me from pestering her daughter and my sister. How could she have known that the act of peering through her binoculars at the orioles nesting in her elms would help fan my spark of interest into a lifelong passion? Because of their efforts, I started down a path from which I have never strayed.

I was fortunate to have grown up in a small town with easy access to nature. My family home was situated between

▲ In the "wilds" of my childhood haunts, fox were regularly seen in spring.

two railway lines, and a walk along either would take me to the mighty Madawaska River. After a hair-raising stroll across one of the towering trestles that spanned this river, I would reach the "wilds" — a long strip of old fields and mixed forest that ran seemingly endlessly in several directions. This area became my personal wilderness, and I explored it at every opportunity. Here, for the first time, I met many wild creatures: skunks, hares, hawks, weasels, owls.... Here, too, in virtual solitude, I polished my skills in luring animals in close. By refining soft "pishing" calls, I was able to draw small birds right up to my face. I learned how to fool Northern Goshawks, Great Horned

Owls, and foxes by mimicking the sounds of injured animals —
loud squeals or squeaks produced by sucking on the backs of my
knuckles.

Some 30 years later, I am still thrilled when a predator
suddenly appears in response to my calls, particularly when
that animal is a wolf.

I was 12 years old when I encountered my first hunter in the
wilds. I was standing on an open section of the river bank,
diligently sucking on the back of my hand, when the tall grasses
ahead began to move. Like the wake that trails an approaching
shark, a swath of swaying grasses cut its way towards me. The
ripple drew nearer and my heart quickened, but still I could not
make out the animal. Suddenly, a
small, brown head followed by a
long, thin body popped out of the
vegetation beside me. As I watched
in nervous elation, a tiny short-
tailed weasel bounded onto my
foot, reared up on its hind legs, and
stared into my eyes. Deciding that I
wasn't worth the effort, it soon
disappeared back into the grasses.

The only wild dogs that lived in
these childhood haunts were a
couple of red foxes. I would happen
upon them infrequently, most often
in early spring as they basked in the
morning sun on south-facing ridges.

▼ Tracks too large for
fox left me wondering
if they might have
been made by a wolf.

On several excursions, including a memorable one illuminated by a January full moon, I came across dog-like prints that seemed far too large to have been made by a fox. I still wonder from time to time if a wandering wolf made those oversized tracks. I never did catch up to their maker, and as a child, I never did see a wolf in the wild.

WOLF HARVESTS

Anti-wolf sentiment has always run deep in the Ottawa Valley, and I saw my fair share of corpses in those early days. Photos of wolf "harvests," which occasionally appeared in the local papers, typically showed a row of wolves hanging lifelessly from a rope strung between two trees or laid out on the snow with a bunch of good old boys standing proudly in the background. At that time, all large canids (the group that includes wolves, foxes, and coyotes) were referred to as "wolves." Many of the unfortunate creatures that were killed were more likely coyotes or "brush wolves," animals much more commonly encountered than true wolves in the semi-open country of my home region.

One of those "good old boys" was a teacher at my elementary school. A notorious wolf-hater, he would occasionally arrive at school with one of his grisly trophies slumped in the back or draped over the hood of his truck. Whenever a dead wolf appeared in the parking lot, we would gather around and, with fearful awe, stare at the menacing teeth and the frozen blood that had spewed out from between them. The misdirected fellow was always ready and eager to elaborate upon the evil ways of these beasts.

▲ With its expanse of forest and northern habitats, and abundance of big game, Algonquin is prime wolf country.

The Summer of 1972

My first real opportunity to meet a wolf in the wild came in the summer of 1972, when I was hired as a summer interpretive naturalist in Algonquin Provincial Park, the wolf capital of eastern North America.

Algonquin Park was a dream come true. Here I was, an enthusiastic young naturalist completely immersed in nature, in one of the wildest and most beautiful parts of Ontario. My job, if you can call it that, was to learn and communicate the wonder of Algonquin's natural history to the park's summer visitors. I was certainly up to the first part of that task!

The park's wildness seemed limitless, and so to spend a whole summer there was nothing short of exhilarating. Everywhere I wandered, I encountered all manner of new and exiting plants and animals. Even the backyard of our staffhouse offered wildlife adventures, for moose and bears occasionally passed through. Of the thousands of animals that called Algonquin home, it was the northern creatures — moose, fishers, Gray Jays, and Spruce Grouse, for example — I especially wanted to see. Naturally, wolves were right at the top of my list.

I was not alone in my desire to find wolves. The Provincial Parks system had more money back then, and there were 12 others sharing the naturalist workload that inaugural summer. Each had their own special interests, but all were more than willing to join the search for wolves as well as share their passion and expertise. I look back at the summer of 1972 as a summer of privilege, one that was the turning point in my life.

Over a month passed after my arrival in the park, and I still had not heard or seen a wolf. As I was to learn, this was not unusual, for wolves are notoriously quiet during the denning season, which stretches from May to July. Not until the dens are abandoned and the pups subsequently moved to open areas known as rendezvous sites do they become at all vocal and willing to respond to human imitations of their howls.

One night in mid-July a group of us ventured down a

portage near Smoke Lake, howling from every rise along the twisting path. Eventually, a long, deep howl rose from the southwest. Although the howl was distant, this was my first wolf experience in the wild. Excitement surged through my body.

A more dramatic encounter took place the following month. One of the naturalists had come across a freshly killed white-tailed deer on the logging road that is now the "bear-nest" branch of the Mizzy Lake Trail. When the rest of us were informed of the find, we could hardly wait for the workday to end so we could slip up to the kill. That evening two jam-packed vehicles set off from the staffhouse after dinner. We bounced our way along the hilly road to get as close to the site as we dared before ditching the trucks. We walked quietly the rest of the distance, not speaking for fear of scaring off the diners. After about a five-minute hike we came upon the carcass, first made obvious by its quite distinctive odor. My notes describe the incident this way:

> We are standing in the dark next to a half-eaten deer, with the stench of death permeating the air. It makes for an eerie experience. The temperature has dropped and we see our breath as we nervously exhale. Overhead, a thousand stars glitter brightly and to the north the green contortions of the aurora set the stage for the dramatic events that soon follow.
>
> We do not have to wait long. Only a few minutes pass when a deep, startlingly close howl breaks the silence. Before it is complete, another howl from a different direction joins in. Then another and another. From all around us the deafening wails of the entire wolf pack saturate the night air. The wolves are so close that in full-blown stereo their howls fill our heads and reverberate between our ears. My body shivers uncontrollably as the howls

 This section of the disused Ottawa, Arnprior, and Parry Sound railway line became a personal retreat.

continue for what seems forever. Then, as suddenly as they had begun, the howls stop. For several moments no one speaks. We cannot, for we are in a state of spiritual intoxication. Eventually, however, the snapping of twigs and rustling of leaves bring us back to reality. Not wanting to keep the hungry animals from their feast any longer, we leave. We are all profoundly moved by the experience.

Later that summer I finally saw a living, breathing, free-ranging wolf. The meeting could not have happened at a better time. I was out howling for wolves with Russ Rutter, a former park naturalist and co-author of the classic book *World of the Wolf*. Russ had a crusty side and at times showed little tolerance for young naturalists. But earlier that summer I and another neophyte naturalist, Bill Crins, had earned his approval by finding Downy Rattlesnake Plantain, a new orchid for the park. As a result, I was occasionally invited along on his outings, such as this wolf-scouting excursion in late August. Ron Tozer and his wife, Pat, completed our search party.

We were driving westbound on Highway 60, with Russ and Ron in the front and Pat and me in the back. We had just rounded the curve beside Brewer Lake when a large, dog-like creature loped across the road in front of us. I am not sure who yelled "wolf!" first, but I do remember grabbing Ron's shoulder in my excitement. Ron remembers this day as well (he claims he still bears the bruises on his shoulder).

Fond memories notwithstanding, I, too, have a permanent memento from that sighting. Russ accommodated my request to record the event in my copy of his book by inscribing:

on the occasion of the sighting of his first wolf by
Mike Runtz at Brewer Lake, Algonquin Park, Aug. 21, 1972.
Witness: R. J. Rutter

Rosie and Wolf Howl Pond

The two following summers, 1973 and 1974, I returned to Algonquin to work once more as a seasonal naturalist. Although I heard wolves on numerous occasions, sightings were few and far between. But until August of 1974 they had never amounted to more than a fleeting glimpse.

I had, by this time, fallen in love with the part of Algonquin bordering the disused railway line that runs between the Arowhon Pines Road and Source Lake. This part of the Ottawa, Arnprior, and Parry Sound Railway had most recently been used as a logging road, but that activity had also ceased by the time I began to explore it. The railway bed cut through a couple of sizable ponds fringed with delicate tamaracks and spindly black spruce. These trees often harboured elusive Boreal Chickadees, affable Gray Jays, and absurdly tame Spruce Grouse. Floating mats of sphagnum moss, alive with carnivorous wildflowers and exotic orchids, covered large sections of the ponds in summer. The moss mats also provided landing platforms for the otters and mink that regularly hunted the ponds, as well as for dozens of basking painted turtles. Numerous dead trees, casualties of water levels raised by the causeways and several beaver dams, stood starkly on the mats and in the shallow waters. These snags added rugged character to the ponds and provided perching and nesting sites for Black-backed Woodpeckers, Tree Swallows, and Olive-sided Flycatchers. By late summer the trees were adorned with thousands of orb-weaver spider webs, which caught the night dew and sparkled in the early morning light. When dawn mists danced among these jeweled spires, the beauty was almost ethereal.

Drawn to the area for its visual splendour, the abundance of northern creatures, and an absence of humans (back then few people visited this area), I made this small piece of Algonquin my personal retreat.

The first of the two ponds was named Wolf Howl Pond, an appropriate appellation as wolves were often heard near the pond. The southwest corner held an open expanse of beaver meadow, which provided an ideal rendezvous site for wolves to use in late summer. Because wolves were heard often, this section of the railway bed became a popular howling location. It was also a great spot for viewing bears, which were attracted to a garbage dump situated to the west of the pond. The dump was operated by a nearby lodge and camp.

One evening as I was driving west from Wolf Howl Pond towards the dump, I spotted a pair of glowing eyes ahead on the railway bed. Excitedly, I realized they belonged to a wolf, not a bear at all! I slammed on the brakes but the animal quickly slinked off the road. I flicked off the headlights and howled out my open window. To my delight the wolf immediately answered back. I waited a minute or two and then pulled on the headlights. There was the wolf back on the road. But it did not stay long and slipped out of view once more. I gave another howl and it answered back. Again, it briefly reappeared on the road. This sequence was repeated several more times until, finally, the wolf remained on the road, clearly illuminated by the truck's headlights. This time when I howled out my open window, it raised its head towards the sky and opened its mouth. I could scarcely stop myself from shouting out, "I am watching a wild wolf howl!"

When it finished howling, the wolf sauntered down the side of the embankment and out of sight. Shaking with excitement, I started up the truck and raced back to the staffhouse to tell anyone who might be still awake of my adventure. I also could not resist telephoning my boss, Chief Park Naturalist Dan Strickland.

Naturally, the temptation to return to the site was too great, but this time I brought some company. We found the wolf with no trouble, and although it did not howl for us, it did something almost as exciting. It squatted down in front of our vehicle and urinated on the road. The wolf's actions also revealed that it was a female.

The wolf remained near the dump for the rest of the summer and co-operated with other staff members who came to see her. She was also encountered farther down on the railway bed, occasionally as far east as West Rose Lake. Because of the wolf's affiliation with this latter location, we took to calling her "Rosie."

Although other staff members got to know her, Rosie was my wolf. I would go up to the old railway every free evening to look for her. Rosie would even appear for me in broad daylight. I can't tell you what an exhilarating experience it was to walk along an old railway bed with a wolf tagging along only 5 metres away. Rosie would follow me just about anywhere, even when I left the trail to walk along the edges of the bog. How I regret not owning a camera then!

I often wondered about what triggered our relationship, but I know it wasn't because of my irresistibly sexy howl. I think Rosie was simply a very lonely wolf. As she was never seen in the company of other wolves, I assumed that she was one of those mythical entities known as a lone wolf. Young wolves separated from the pack are occasionally encountered in the fall, but other lone wolves are social outcasts, unwanted by other groups. In either case, a lone wolf is usually doomed, for without help in hunting large game, it usually cannot survive on its own. But Rosie was able to scrounge enough scraps from the

The famous Rosie is seen here visiting Ron Pittaway's feeder at the staffhouse (PHOTO: RON PITTAWAY).

Most wolf sightings consist of a fleeting glimpse of one loping across the road or trail.

dump to keep her going, at least until the fall, when the camps and lodge shut down and no more refuse was sent to the dump. With this supply of free and easy food gone, unless she could find a pack of wolves that would allow her to join them, Rosie's fate seemed sealed.

That winter Ron Pittaway, one of the seasonal naturalists, stayed behind to work in the park. He lived in the staffhouse, where along with a feeder for the birds, he maintained a tray of table scraps for mammals. Fox, marten, and even the occasional fisher made nocturnal forays to pick off the meat. One day, to Ron's delight, another visitor showed up. In her desperate wanderings to find food, Rosie had stumbled across his feeder.

Thanks to Ron's efforts, Rosie survived the winters of 1974 and 1975. Over those years she made a couple of appearances in a nearby campground, where she was seen pilfering scraps from garbage cans. Although no one is sure of the exact day Rosie disappeared for good, there is a story circulating that one day the enterprising wolf came upon a campsite offering a little more than the paltry fare she was used to. There, tied to a post by its leash, was a scrumptious poodle. The leash and post remained untouched, but the little doggie disappeared. Oddly enough, so did Rosie, never to be seen again! At least, this is how the story goes.

It's rare to encounter any wolf, let alone a tame one. Only a handful of others like Rosie have been reported during the 100-plus years of the park's existence. I have met three others, one of which behaved in a most peculiar way.

Chapter 2

A FEW BOLD WOLVES

To see a wolf, even briefly, is always exciting; to have one dauntlessly approach you is a somewhat unsettling experience. One of my closest and most bizarre meetings with a wolf took place in April 1992. I was driving south on the Opeongo Road when I spotted a wolf running along the road towards me. I hit the brakes and grabbed for my camera, praying the animal would not bolt and disappear into the woods. Fortunately, it kept coming. In fact, it ran right past my truck door. I scrambled out of the vehicle, tripod and camera in tow, dropped to my knees, and frantically tried to attach the camera's quick mount to the tripod head. By the time my fumbling fingers had snapped the parts together, the wolf had travelled some distance and was rapidly moving away. I framed the wolf in the camera lens and desperately tried to get its attention by howling at it. To my delight it halted, but after a quick glance over its shoulder it continued on its way. Howling failed to arouse its interest a second time, so I tried to imitate an injured animal's squeal by sucking on my knuckles. The wolf ignored this, too. Then, for some baffling reason, I started to make a loud "beep, beep, beep" sound, which did the trick. The wolf stopped dead in its tracks and turned completely around. I continued to make this weird noise and with both hands flapped my coat open and closed (don't ask me why I did

 By howling at it, I was able to make this wolf stop and look back.

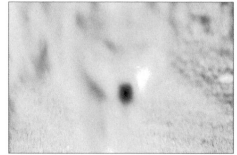

ABOVE: The wolf was moving so rapidly it soon moved in too close for me to focus.

LEFT: When I inexplicably flapped my coat and went "beep-beep-beep," the wolf began to run towards me.

this; I really have no idea). Surprisingly, the wolf suddenly began to lope towards me.

My heart racing with excitement, I tried to focus my camera lens on the wolf's face — which was incredibly difficult under the circumstances. The rapidly approaching wolf grew larger and larger in the viewfinder. My photographic efforts always seemed to be one lens twist behind the wolf's head (in fact, this was the case, as I discovered when the slides were processed). When the animal's face completely filled the frame, I figured it was time to retreat into the truck, so I abandoned my gear and grabbed the door. Just as I shut the door the wolf arrived. It stopped beside the vehicle and stood there, a couple of metres away, staring at me somewhat quizzically. After a few moments it turned and continued on its original route. I jumped out of the vehicle and tried to regain its attention. Again, it ignored my howls but responded immediately to my strange beeping. Once more I tried — with limited success — to photograph the wolf as it bore down on me. I retreated into the vehicle only when the wolf got too close for comfort.

This scenario was played out a third time, with one major difference. This time I spent a second too many looking through the camera and the wolf arrived before I could get the truck door open. Using the tripod as a shield, I gently kept the animal away. This wasn't too difficult. Despite its approach, the wolf showed absolutely no sign of aggression: its ears were not laid back nor its teeth bared. Nevertheless, I was somewhat afraid. While the wolf pushed against my tripod legs, I looked at the animal for any sign of illness, such as frothing at the mouth. (Even though rabies is extremely rare in wolves, this was the first concern that sprang to mind.) The only slightly odd aspects of its appearance were a somewhat vacant look to the eyes and a virtually non-existent belly where it joined the back haunches. Perhaps the wolf was in a state of starvation, which would certainly account for its being somewhat out of sorts. But why it reacted so swiftly to my odd beeps and not to my injured prey squeals, a sound that usually holds strong appeal for a hungry animal, was puzzling. I had a whimsical and facetious thought: I wondered whether the wolf had a previous bad experience with a researcher's radio transmitter. If so, this might explain its apparent dislike of my beeping.

After a minute or two the wolf continued on its way. I watched it trot up the road until it was out of sight.

Encounters Between Wolves and Campers

▲ Bold wolves usually express indifference, not aggression, towards campers.

Does a wolf that has lost its fear of humans become aggressive, thus posing a real threat to humans? In a couple of recent cases, unusually bold Algonquin wolves did, in fact, injure campers (and were consequently destroyed). Although another conclusion might easily be drawn, an examination of the circumstances surrounding these isolated incidents indicates that the wolves harboured no ill intent towards the campers.

For several months before the first incident, which occurred on August 9, 1987, an unusually bold wolf had been seen wandering along the highway and through a couple of campgrounds. On this particular day in August, it appeared in the Whitefish Group Campground. After being chased around by some boys, the wolf walked up to a girl sitting by a campfire. Sensing something behind her, the girl swung around and shone her flashlight to see what was there. The wolf, undoubtedly as startled as the girl was, instinctively grabbed the arm pointing at its face. It clamped down for only a moment, then released and continued on its way. The girl sustained only a small scratch from the wolf's teeth, which had barely broken her skin under her sweater. A wolf's jaws are so powerful, they are capable of breaking a deer's leg — an object considerably more substantial than a child's arm. It is quite apparent that the wolf had no intention of harming the girl; it only acted on instinct when the arm wielding the light unexpectedly appeared in its face.

As a precaution, the girl was given anti-rabies shots. The wolf, on the other hand, received shots of a much different nature. After it was disposed of, it was examined for rabies. To no great surprise, it tested negative.

A number of us had met this same wolf earlier in the summer when we had been out howling. When it approached us, we quickly retreated into our vehicle. On one occasion it jumped up and put its feet on the truck window. Another time it chewed the bumper of a car. While it displayed unusually tame and bold behaviour, it was never really aggressive.

A few years later, in 1994, another bold wolf appeared near Opeongo Lake. This wolf was a little more aggressive than the Whitefish wolf and would approach canoeists walking the portage trails. It would growl and grab their packsacks on the ground. Eventually it nipped a young boy and, a few weeks later, a woman. When the wolf was finally destroyed, it too tested negative for rabies.

I am quite sure that I met this animal earlier in the year but much further east. A wolf had shown up at Radiant Lake and began to steal food from a bear trap (a big live trap used to capture and transport "problem" bears). Park staff operating the trap began to feed the wolf by tossing it doughnuts and other foods. Eventually it could be hand-fed. At a nearby logging camp the feeding cycle continued. Late that spring the wolf was seen travelling along a logging road in the general direction of Opeongo Lake. Since the "nuisance" wolf showed up at Opeongo after the Radiant animal disappeared, it seems likely they were the one and the same. It may well be that by feeding the wolf, the people at Radiant Lake had sentenced it to death.

The most recent episode involving a bold wolf took place in August 1996, when an animal actually inflicted fairly serious facial wounds on a young boy. Unfortunately, the incident has been greatly exaggerated, with one version stating that the boy was dragged out of his sleeping bag and half-eaten. The boy's family was camping under the stars without a tent when a wolf entered their campsite, grabbed the boy's head, and dragged him a short distance. While it might appear that the wolf intentionally attacked the boy (the boy's face was torn), evidence suggests the wolf may have tugged at the bag first, only grabbing the boy after trying for a new grip on the material.

Bold wolves have been known to grab pillows and other items from under the heads of sleeping humans and yet not bite the people. It is possible that the boy's head happened to be in the wrong place at the wrong time. If the boy had been lying the other way, quite possibly his feet would have been grabbed by the wolf. Reports that trickled in later support the theory that the wolf had no design on the boy. Park staff learned that the same animal had been encountered in previous weeks by other campers and had dragged around their personal possessions. During the period when staff were searching for the wolf, it visited other campers, stealing the pillow from beneath one man who was sleeping under the stars. If the earlier encounters

ALGONQUIN'S "BOLD" WOLVES

Virtually all of the bold wolves have been sighted in the south-central part of Algonquin, many quite close to Highway 60. And in that area these encounters seem to be on the increase. The first "tame" wolf frequented the Mew Lake area in 1963. Then there was Rosie in the mid-1970s, the 1987 wolf at the Whitefish Group Campground, and the 1996 animal at Tom Thomson Lake. In addition, there have been approachable wolves near Brule Lake in 1990, the Opeongo Road in 1992, Pog and Rock Lakes in 1993, Mew and Opeongo Lakes in 1994, and, most recently, near Mew Lake in early 1997.

had been reported, the unfortunate mishap with the boy might have been prevented. Regardless, this wolf was destroyed and, as in all other cases where the wolves were tested, no evidence of rabies was found.

Why Bold Wolves?

It is clear that the boldness exhibited by a few Algonquin wolves has not been due to the deranging effects of rabies. Why then are some wolves unusually tame? Why have Algonquin's bold wolves been found in the park's south-central section? And are bold wolves becoming more frequent? While there may be no simple answers to these questions, there are a few plausible explanations.

One is that in every animal population there are a few individuals that behave differently. This being the case, over the span of a hundred years one might expect there to have been a few bold wolves in Algonquin. And with park visitation up dramatically from the early years, much of it concentrated in the south-central part of the park, odds are greater that these aberrant

Even in Algonquin, wolves can pay a steep price for interacting with humans.

individuals would have been encountered by humans in that region.

Also, some wild animals are bound to become accustomed to humans and gradually lose their fear in any park visited by millions of people. This has certainly proven true for chipmunks, raccoons, and even moose.

But I think other factors are also at play. Throughout most of their worldwide range, wolves have always feared humans — and for very good reason. They were once considered villainous killers, and people used guns, snares, and poison to try to exterminate them. Attitudes slowly began to change, however, and 65 years after the park's establishment, wolves in Algonquin came to be protected. A moratorium on wolf-killing was in effect from 1958 to 1963 while a research program was conducted, then in 1964 and 1965, the final two years of the study, wolves were shot as a means of data collection for population demographics. Thus, in terms of continuous protection, Algonquin wolves have enjoyed little more than three decades of sanctuary.

The same cannot be said for Algonquin wolves that venture outside the park. Packs with territories stretching beyond Algonquin, or ones that follow deer to their wintering sites in adjacent lowlands, for the most part continue to meet a gauntlet of guns and snares. But wolves born into packs whose territories are more centrally situated in Algonquin may be less likely to experience these threats. Perhaps in this region of Algonquin, the protection, along with the increased contact between wolves and park users (about half a million people visit Algonquin annually), has created a few bold wolves.

While these two pack members stayed back, one of the dominant pair came in to challenge me. Unfortunately, the camera system jammed and the moment went unrecorded.

Wolf Barking

Aggression is an important component of the wolf's social structure. It is not so much the expression of aggression but rather the threat of it that is used to maintain hierarchy. Rank is established by dominance, and dominance stems from size and strength. Wolves begin to establish their social status at an early age through aggressive play. I have watched pups at late summer rendezvous sites tumble around trying to gain a physical advantage over one another, and the growling, snarling, and yelping can be quite fearsome. In such interactions, the loser submits by either running away or lying on its back. Throughout their lives, wolves continue to act out roles of dominance and submission.

Vocally, wolves can announce their aggressive intent by barking. A bark can be used to warn an intruding wolf that it is time to leave. The first encounter I had with a barking wolf was in November 1987. I was driving along the Sand Lake Road on the east side of Algonquin looking for animal signs. Where the road runs beneath the power lines, I spotted fresh wolf droppings. When I got out and howled, an entire pack of wolves responded right away. My notes from the time read:

The wolves are just past the power line cut and not far off the road. I drive up as close as possible to their approximate location and howl again. They answer from somewhere near a grassy clearing beyond a fringe of trees that borders the road. I quietly walk down to the opening, carefully treading on wet moss and lichens to avoid making noise. By the number of trails that wind their way through the grasses, I know the wolves have been here for a while. Judging by the shrieks of ravens, I figure a kill must have been made just beyond the far end of the clearing. With pounding heart, I squeeze against a small pine growing at the edge of the grasses. Once hidden and with my camera lens pointing towards the screaming birds, I howl. Only seconds pass before two wolves appear, walking along the far edge of the clearing. They climb on top of an old log and stare in my general direction. Seconds later a larger wolf comes into view and cuts across the middle of the grassy swale. Within about nine metres of me, it sits down and howls. With shaking fingers I point my camera and soon have a frame-filling view of its howling face. But when I squeeze the trigger release on the gun stock, to my horror nothing happens. The cable release has jammed. Here I am, with a beautiful wolf in plain view, howling away, and my camera refuses to function. After it finishes its howl, the wolf gives a couple of rough barks and saunters into the woods. It circles around behind me, still not sure as to where the intruding "wolf" is, and barks a couple of more times. It must have caught my scent trail then, for it becomes completely silent. After about a minute I see movement at the end of the opening and catch a glimpse of the wolf heading back.

Since that memorable day, I have heard wolves bark to silence pups and to draw them away from potential danger. Most often, however, barks seem to be used to warn a perceived intruder to leave the area. Usually these warnings consist of a couple of gruff barks, but on a number of occasions I have heard really aggressive barking.

Ten years ago, while I was in the company of two fellow park employees, I had an early August encounter on Highway 60 near Eos Lake. I had stopped to howl for wolves late one night on my way back to the staffhouse. After a few single howls, a group of pups answered to the north of the highway. While I was enjoying their wild music, I heard a loud crashing in the woods directly behind me. The night was extremely dark, clouds obscured any star or moonlight, and though I could not make out the animal, I suspected a wolf was coming in to check me out. The crashing continued until the animal reached the edge of the woods. The noise stopped, but I wondered if the animal might still be approaching on the moss-covered rocks. Silence for several moments, until a mechanical whine announced the approach of a truck on the highway. As the sound neared, the vehicle's headlights appeared over the top of a rise to the west. The beams slowly descended towards me as the truck cleared the hill, until they finally fell across the pavement in front of me, illuminating the far side of the highway. There, just past the far shoulder of the road, stood a magnificent wolf on a low rock cut. As I watched, it tilted its head back and let loose a deep, short howl. It then barked a couple of times and retreated into the forest when the truck neared.

Ecstatic, I drove back to the staffhouse to relay my experience to the other summer naturalists and invite them to come back with me to look for the wolf. Most of the staff members had never seen a wolf, but this didn't prevent one of the returning naturalists — who fancied himself an expert — from loudly announcing, "Once a wolf sees a person, that's it, it won't show itself again, and you [meaning me] should know that about wolves!" Well, I guess I did not know that. Back I went, accompanied by two others, Don Tyreman and Sharon O'Neill. As soon as we arrived at Eos Lake, I promptly howled. No response, not even from the pups. Additional howls, including a couple of group efforts, failed to elicit any type of reaction and, dejectedly, I began to wonder if the young expert back at the staffhouse may have been right after all. Just before giving up for good, I decided to scan the area quickly with the flashlight. Shining back at us from some distance down the highway was a set of white eyes. There was the wolf, just sitting on the road. We had not heard its approach because it had been walking on the pavement. I switched off the flashlight and howled. This time it answered back. With me leading the way, the three of us quietly edged closer, stepping gingerly to avoid making too much noise and scaring the wolf.

As we approached in the pitch-dark night, I kept howling softly. The wolf responded with a howl and a couple of gruff barks. I, too, barked, and lo and behold, the wolf, hidden by the darkness, began to bark aggressively non-stop. It sounded like a deranged attack dog in an action movie. Its sharp, deep barks continued for as much as two minutes, then along came a vehicle. When its lights struck the wolf, the animal barked

IF YOU ARE APPROACHED BY A WOLF

These days when a wolf approaches me, I don't bark at it, because this may upset it unnecessarily. I enjoy the brief encounter, then let the animal go on its way. Like all wild animals, wolves deserve our respect. It is a rare privilege to meet a wolf, and we must always appreciate that.

Although wolves are aggressive by nature, they rarely display this behaviour to humans. Still, while they do not present any real threat, the occasional wolf may behave differently than most. It is best to err on the side of caution if you do encounter a wolf that seems rather bold and approachable. Try to frighten it away, not encourage it, and if it is at all aggressive, leave it alone and report your encounter to the park staff immediately.

With so few bold wolves ever encountered in Algonquin, odds are that you will never meet one. It is likely that most Algonquin wolves will continue to possess a deep-rooted fear of humans. For this reason alone, they will remain creatures of mystery.

▲ Bold wolves are extremely rare. Most wolves will remain creatures of mystery, vanishing into the shadows long before you are aware of their presence.

gruffly one more time before vanishing into the forest.

I had brought along a tape recorder this second time around in the hope of capturing the wolf's howl, which had been so dramatically close earlier. Few people have ever heard, let alone recorded, the aggressive warning barks of a wolf. You can imagine how painfully disappointed I was when I discovered that, in my elation, I had forgotten to turn on the recorder.

The moment had transfixed us all. When I flicked on the flashlight and swung around to Don and Sharon, to my surprise, they were both as pale as ghosts. Sharon was locked onto Don's arm so tightly that, I swear, days later Don's arm still bore five little imprints from her frantic grip. Sharon confided to me later that she had never before been as frightened. Come to think of it, I guess I probably hadn't either!

 Dens are often dug where the soil is softer, such as in this abandoned sandpit.

 This den, its entrance under a fallen pine, was in the ruins of an old homestead.

C h a p t e r 3

THE WOLVES OF SUMMER

In Algonquin, most wolf encounters take place during the latter part of summer. There are two good reasons for this: visits to the park generally coincide with summer vacations, and wolves are particularly vocal at this time of year. While it is charming to surmise that Algonquin wolves are co-operative animals generously saving their voices until the park is full of appreciative listeners, the timing is pure coincidence. The inclination to howl in late summer is due solely to a dramatic seasonal change in the wolves' behaviour.

S p r i n g

i n t h e D e n

Wolves are difficult to hear before the middle of July. The period of near-silence begins in spring, prior to the birth of the pups (usually four to six pups are born in a litter) in late April or May. Like their closest relatives, foxes and coyotes, female wolves give birth in underground dens. The wolf dens I have seen were in a variety of locations: at the bottom of a hill bordering a beaver meadow; in an abandoned sandpit; on a slope beside a forested stream; and in the remains of an old homestead's root cellar. Other Algonquin dens have also been found under tree roots and fallen slabs of rocks.

One den, whose exact location eluded me, was situated on a steep, boulder-covered hillside alongside McRainey Lake. It was late May and I was alone in my canoe, quietly paddling over the mirror-like water just as the sun was coming up on the horizon. An adult wolf howled unexpectedly from the top of a large hill on the southwest shore of the lake. To my delight, a second adult and a group of pups joined in. As the pups would have been a month old at best, I knew they had to be howling from the den. I drifted along, pondering the den's location as I savoured the magnificent dawn chorus echoing between the steep hills embracing the lake. A few minutes passed and one of the adults howled again, this time from much farther away. As if they were saying goodbye, the other adult and the pups called back from their hidden location on the hillside. While they were howling, I quickly canoed towards them, my paddle never leaving the water to prevent the sound of water dripping off its blade. When the wolves completed their salutations, I stayed my paddle and glided in silence towards the shore. Careful not to bang my old Peterborough on the rocks, I lightly stepped out and lifted the canoe onto solid ground. After a few anxious minutes, I howled softly. A cacophony of yips, yelps, barks, and baby howls from the pups erased any fear I had that the wolves had seen me.

While they were calling, I cautiously ventured up the boulder-strewn slope. Each excited step drew me closer, but I still couldn't see the wolves, even though they were only a couple of hundred metres away at most. I continued up the hillside. Just when it seemed that at any second I would come upon them, a loud bark silenced the group. I had been spotted. Substituting speed for stealth, I dashed up to where it seemed the howls and bark originated, confident the den would be there. Five minutes went by, and still I had failed to turn up even one clue as to its location. Not wishing to disturb the animals any more, I reluctantly abandoned my efforts and returned to my canoe. Although undeniably a little disappointed, overall I was quite exhilarated by the experience.

The Rendezvous Site

For almost three months the wolf pups are in dens, but by the middle of the summer they have grown considerably and are too big for their subterranean quarters. Eventually, the dens are abandoned and the pups taken to new and spacious summer "homes." Here, above ground, the pups enter the second phase of their lives.

Post-den pup-rearing sites share three essential characteristics: they are always in open terrain, commonly a bog or a grassy opening (like the meadows growing in dried-up beaver ponds); coniferous cover, usually spruce or firs, borders the open area; and water is close at hand.

The pups remain near these open areas while the rest of the pack goes off hunting. After making a kill, the adults gobble

By mid-July the dens are abandoned and the pups moved to new locations known as rendezvous sites. All the rendezvous sites I have seen include an open area surrounded by conifers and access to water.

down chunks of the meat and return to the post-den site. Immediately upon its return, a food-bearer is swarmed by the pups, which make it regurgitate the food by tugging at the corners of its mouth. I like to refer to this feeding routine as "meals on heels!" Because the pups and adults routinely reconvene at these late summer sites, they are known as rendezvous sites.

From mid-July to the middle of autumn, wolf packs typically will use a number of rendezvous sites. Usually, any one site is used from several days to several weeks, but on occasion residence is established for a longer period. One wolf pack I kept contact with occupied a rendezvous site along the Oxtongue River for three months.

As if celebrating liberation from their natal dens, wolves become characteristically vocal in their late summer haunts. Night after night and sometimes during the day, packs can be heard howling from the rendezvous sites. The deep howls of an adult or two often accompany the spirited, high-pitched chorus of the pups; at times, only the youngsters can be heard. While the latter scenario may suggest that pups are occasionally left unattended, it has been my experience that an adult is never far away.

One August evening about 10 years ago, I was listening to a group of pups camped out in an old gravel pit. There were growls and snarls aplenty as the young wolves sorted their who's who in the puppy world. I decided to sneak closer, so I got them to howl to cloak my approach. As I was working my way towards them, from the east a distant adult howled twice. I raised the pups a second time and the lone adult answered again, this time from about only half its original distance.

While the pups were noisily calling, I descended the steep embankment and entered the pit. Although I couldn't make out the animals in the dark (it was an overcast night), I could hear them running around and playing not far from me. At one point some fairly fearsome puppy growls and yelps broke out. I never discovered what the scuffle was all about because the activity ended abruptly when a large animal bounded down the far slope of the pit, scattering stones in every direction. A loud bark confirmed my suspicion that the distant adult had returned to protect the youngsters. A second loud bark summoned the now-silent pups, which quickly raced off into the darkness, their guardian close behind.

I returned the next night to check on the wolves' whereabouts and was delighted when they howled back from a creek system not far to the east. Since I do not make it a habit to walk into rendezvous sites at any time of day — this was the only time that I have ever walked (or ever will walk) into a site in the middle of the night — I was relieved that my earlier intrusion had caused the pack to move only a short distance.

Adult wolves do not always respond when we howl near a rendezvous site, but I believe that they regularly come in to check us out. We are just not aware of it. On a number of occasions, particularly at night, I have heard an animal walking in the woods after I had howled. Once in a while a wolf will show itself, confirming my suspicions as to the origin of the sounds. Adult wolves have even come in to investigate my howls during the day. A dramatic example of this occurred on Highway 60 near West Smith Lake late one August.

I was passing by that area with two friends en route to look for Spruce Grouse. I knew a pack of wolves had been heard near the lake and as my friends had not heard wolves for years, I stopped. It was a little past six, and the sun was not yet up. A beautiful late August mist was rising from the lake and shrouding most of the highway. I encouraged Brian and Jacquie to howl, hoping they would have the pleasure of raising a response on their own. Despite several singles and a group howl, however, no wolves answered back. So I was asked to give it a go. Sure enough, the pups responded wonderfully from down by the lake. As we were enjoying their wild music, a loud crashing came from the hardwood hill behind us on the opposite side of the highway. I motioned to my friends to be still, and we quietly stood and waited. The crashing came in spurts. The animal would take a few steps down the hill, then stop, probably to listen and sniff the air for the intruding wolves. This went on for a minute or so, until the animal reached the edge of the forest. Then silence. Perhaps the animal was walking on the moss-covered rocks that lay between the edge of the forest and the road.

We stared in silent anticipation towards the small, scattered spruce and firs that grew just beyond the shoulder of the road. Suddenly, from between two low spruces a large grey head came looming into the mist. Instinctively, my friends pointed and whispered excitedly, "There it is!" In response, the wolf barked and pulled back out of sight. We could hear it crashing as it retreated into the safety of the forest. I howled a couple of times and the wolf howled and barked back. It then paced back and forth along the edge of the forest, finally moving off more to the west. Once again its footsteps fell silent, as if it were walking on softer ground. Sure enough, the wolf came back out to the road, this time about a hundred metres farther down the road. It stood on a rock by the shoulder of the road and, in full view, howled. Then it trotted across the highway, stopping briefly to show its indignation by squatting and urinating (thereby revealing its female gender). Having reaffirmed her territorial rights, the wolf continued down the slope towards the lake to join her pups.

Over the years, I have gone in to rendezvous sites on several

In the early part of summer Algonquin wolves feed primarily on white-tailed deer. Adults bring ingested meat back to the pups at the rendezvous site.

occasions in the early morning — well before sunrise — to observe and photograph wolves. It takes a great deal of effort and a large dose of luck to approach a pack without their knowledge. The slightest sound, the briefest flash of movement, even the faintest aroma of soap can erase any chance of sighting a wolf. To improve my odds, I don't shower for days and wear the same unwashed clothes for weeks. While I may not make new friends, I do manage to see the occasional wolf.

I also make it a point to go alone. Only once, to my regret, did I bring along someone else. It was early October and I had just finished prepping my companion on how to behave when

Meandering streams that wind their way through beaver meadows
make for superb rendezvous sites as well as general travel corridors.

 Algonquin's rugged landscape is perfect wolf country.

Algonquin wolves are beautiful animals, displaying a rich cinnamon on their snout, ears, neck, and thighs.

The cavalcade of cars heading for the howling site is an impressive spectacle.

Since wolves often travel forest access roads, these are excellent places to look for their signs.

Clusters of butterflies, especially Tiger Swallowtails, often reveal the presence of scats.

Wolves and moose share the same habitat and even interact. Prime bulls are rarely, if ever, attacked by Algonquin wolves, however.

 Wolves easily blend into the landscape, disappearing usually long before we are aware of their presence.

 My hours of waiting were rewarded by first two, then three pups scrambling down the slope by the old stump.

 Beavers are an important food for wolves, particularly in late summer and fall when the beavers are creating food piles and in early spring when they leave the water in search of fresh food.

Few Algonquin visitors actually see a wolf. Most meet their first wolves by hearing them on a Public Wolf Howl.

Without wolves, we have no wilderness, and without wilderness, we have nothing.

▲ By mid-October the pups look like the adults and will·
soon be abandoning the rendezvous sites to travel
with the pack.

entering the rendezvous site, which was along a creek just south
of Lake Louisa. I stressed how we might have to stand
completely motionless for an hour or more if we hoped to see a
wolf.

The excursion started off well. We had successfully snuck
along a creek to the edge of an old beaver meadow, not making
any perceptible noise. Separated by about 30 metres, we took
cover behind some alders. Half an hour later I howled, and no
response for a minute or so. Then a flash of movement to my
right. A beautiful adult wolf, probably one of the dominant pair,
had come in to check out the intruder. When I had howled, I had

BLOOD, SWEAT, AND TEARS

I rarely visit a rendezvous site, but when I do, a great deal of planning goes into the expedition. After locating wolves by their howls, I try to determine the lay of the land and the location of the site by examining aerial photographs. Then, the next morning, an hour or two before sunrise, I start my painstaking trek. Whenever possible, I access the site by wading in shallow streams or following moose trails, which generally make for the easiest and quietest approaches. I move slowly, each step deliberate and carefully placed. I stop frequently and intently listen for any wolf sound. It's an excruciating pace, and I am fortunate if I am able to advance half a kilometre in an hour.

When I finally reach the rendezvous site, I look for the best vantage point and warily make my way to it. Setting up a manufactured blind would be impossible, so I quietly hide myself in natural cover. Then the wait begins.

Sitting completely motionless for several hours is never an easy or particularly enjoyable task, but those who wish to observe wolves must pay their dues. Cramped muscles are, however, only part of the admission price. Ravenous insects quickly seek you out, and because you are not wearing repellents (the super-sensitive noses of wolves would detect the repellent long before the insects do), you must suffer their annoying bites. And wiping the hordes of annoying creatures away from your face is not an option either, as any type of movement would soon alert a wolf to your presence. The only thing you can do is sit and suffer.

> With all the effort and discomfort, there is still no guarantee that you will see wolves. If even one pack member catches your scent or otherwise detects you, all the animals vanish. Or you may walk in to the wrong site. Or the wolves may already be gone, having changed rendezvous sites overnight.

thrown my voice to the north, and the wolf intently stared in that direction. My eyes shifted over to my companion, but he had not seen the wolf. Then, horrified, I saw him turn far too quickly as he glanced around the meadow. My eyes moved back over to the wolf, but fortunately it hadn't seen my friend's movement. It started to walk out from behind the alders and headed towards an opening where my camera was pointed. The lighting was dramatic and I excitedly got ready to press the cable release. But just before the wolf walked out into plain view, it suddenly stopped dead in its tracks and looked straight at my friend. I glanced over to see him put his hand in his pocket. A jingle of coin and the wolf was gone. A few minutes later we watched seven wolves walk along an old alder-covered dam at the opposite end of the beaver meadow, heading away from us. Our wolf-watching and photographic endeavours were done, short-changed you might say by an error in judgment.

I am used to unsuccessful ventures, especially those involving one of the most elusive creatures of the wild. Few outings have been as physically demanding as my tromp into North Bog just south of Opeongo Lake.

Costello Creek failed to provide access to North Bog.

It was mid-September, and I had heard the howls of a distant pack to the southwest of Opeongo Lake. I figured the wolves were somewhere near a large sphagnum opening known as North Bog. A perusal of aerial photographs of this area indicated there were only two feasible routes to access the bog, one along a stream that flowed from the south end of the bog into Costello Creek, the other a potentially strenuous bushwhack over a considerable height of land. Since a paddle of less than a kilometre was required to reach the stream access, I checked out that option first. The following notes were taken in the canoe as I explored this possible route:

As I paddled along this beautiful creek, Shadow Darner dragonflies kept me company.

At first the paddling is easy but soon the water becomes shallow. Twice I run aground on a log and have to pole my canoe over it. At other times the pondweeds are so thick they almost wrench the paddle from my hand. After about 20 minutes I stop paddling and howl. Only a distant raven screams back. A burst of welcome breeze pushes my canoe along the creek. To my left, a shadow darner, a large blue, green, and black dragonfly, courses the edge of the creek. I pick up my paddle and travel farther down the creek.

In the water to my right, a sudden movement catches my eye. A mink frog, its mottled black and green back only inches beneath the surface, kicks its way under a raft of water-shield leaves. At this time of year, these leaves resemble an abstract work of art, for they are full of meandering lines chewed by Donacia beetle larvae. Besides food for beetles, water-shield is also a favourite sodium-rich dish of moose.

The creek twists and turns like a sidewinder making its way across hot sand. After a few more bends are navigated I stop and howl. A Gray Jay's mellow whistle draws my attention to a clump of black spruce over which a medium-sized bird flies. But it is not a jay, for its wings are too long and pointed. With binoculars I make it out to be a small falcon. A flash of red as its tail fans and a male kestrel lands on a tall dead tree.

A couple of more curves and the creek brings me to a maze of partly submerged tree trunks. I try to run over the first of these but get stuck. After freeing my canoe I decide to turn back. The canoeing is now quite difficult and I still have not heard any wolves.

It turned out that even if I had heard wolves, I would not have been able to reach them from the water route. The small creek flowing from North Bog did not hold enough water for a canoe

For a couple of hours I watched North Bog through the poplars on this hill. Here, I was startled by a loud crashing, which, as it turned out, was caused by a bear.

to pass through. It was also so choked with alders that an approach on foot was out of the question. But this all seemed academic for I was not even sure that there were wolves in North Bog. To try to locate them one last time, I returned later that night and howled from the road. To my surprise the pack answered back from the exact same direction from which they had responded the previous night. I decided to access North Bog via the overland route the next morning.

Although this route did not contain any alder thickets, it did offer one major obstacle — an inordinately high hill. The height of land was going to be even more trying this particular trip because of unseasonably warm temperatures. It was already 20 degrees Celsius when I began my predawn climb, 20-odd kilograms of camera gear strapped to my back. The notes I made that day best describe the expedition in its proper detail:

While strenuous enough, the climb proved to be less difficult than anticipated despite the bog lying on the opposite side of a rather onerous hill. Perhaps the many months of conditioning have paid off. No doubt this same route would have done me in first thing this past spring!

I am sitting on the elevated crest of the hill, North Bog visible through the crowns of the towering poplars that line the west side of the slope. It is a huge bog, and I can only see a small part of it from this vantage point. The sun has long risen, as has the temperature. I have been here for at least an hour and a half now and have not yet seen any sign of wolves. My thoughts are abruptly interrupted by a series of dull thuds and a subsequent crash just to my right. I peer down through the jungle of bracken and sweet-fern but can see nothing. Minutes pass and only a cicada's buzz breaks the silence. It is always a bit spooky when you know a large animal is nearby but you cannot see it. Judging by the nature of the sound and a fresh cavity in the ground that I find when I eventually wander along the slope, I conclude that a foraging bear has dislodged a large rock, which then rolled down the hill.

I return to my perch and resume my watch over the bog. Although I am not moving, because of the heat and the earlier excitement, sweat drips steadily off my brow. Another half hour or so passes and I decide to venture down to the bog for a closer look. I hoist my gear over my shoulder and start the descent. The transition from dry forest slope to flat, waterlogged bog is sudden, with only a narrow but dense belt of fir and spruces separating the two. I am surprised that the leatherleaf in the bog is not exceptionally high or thick and that luxurious chunks of sphagnum moss show through it everywhere. The bog is an old one and the transformation from pond to forest is advancing. Sentinels of small trees, mainly black spruce and tamarack with a few white pines, stand guard over the mat.

▲ This vast expanse of sphagnum moss and leatherleaf is known as North Bog. The wolves were on the far side of the hill visible at the far end of the bog.

Suspecting that the wolves might be sheltering in the shade of the tall black spruce lining the outlet at the south end of the bog, I sneak towards the middle of the bog where I will hide in a small group of white pines. The walk to these trees is for the most part quite pleasant. The thick sphagnum, ranging in colour from a deep red to a pleasing pink, cushions my feet as if I am walking on a plush carpet. Occasionally, I must push through a thick patch of leatherleaf but I feel confident that the wind, now quite strong, is covering any noise I generate.

I reach the pines and push my tripod as close as possible to one of the trunks. Sitting on top of a cushiony mound of moss in the cool shade of the pine, I wonder what the wolves are up to. Did they spot me crossing the open bog? Or are they sleeping in the shade of the spruces, waiting for the burning sun to slip out of sight? I am tempted to howl to find out exactly where they are but I decide to wait until the light is less harsh for photography. Also, the pups may well venture on their own to play, so it is prudent to wait. They will probably not appear for a while, for the sun is burning with the same intensity as yesterday (the previous day the mercury rose to 32 degrees Celsius) and the mat is acting like a solar reflector.

As I sit on my moss cushion, listening to the blue bottle flies buzz around me, I wonder how many humans have ever set foot in this beautiful bog. Because it is off the beaten path, with no hiking trails leading to it or canoeable waters flowing through it, probably only a handle at most. To my knowledge it was first "discovered" by Dan Strickland, pursuing his life's passion — looking for Gray Jays. "Discover" is a word I find amusing. Whenever we humans stumble across something of interest we claim to have discovered it. This is in spite of the discovery having been there for thousands of years and being paid myriad visits by wolves and many other wild creatures! Anyway, it seems rather fitting that it was Dan who first heard this pack of wolves howl here a few nights ago.

Feeling a bit weary from the efforts of the past two days, I lay down in the shade of the pine. The moss and leatherleaf make a comfortable bed, one hidden from the eyes of any wolf. Using my camera backpack as a pillow, I doze off. I awake some time later to the wheezy calls of a Boreal Chickadee, the northern cousin of the Black-capped. Then I feel something walking on my face, and on my hands and chest. I glance down to see ants. Lots of ants! I guess I have lain on top of an ant mound for these insects are climbing all over me. I carefully knock them off my clothes and skin, even picking the odd one out from inside my pants. After I am satisfied I have them off me, I slowly raise my head and glance around. Nothing but the same old bog scene. The sky has changed, though, with a wispy sheet of cloud rising from the south. This heat has to break soon, so perhaps this is the first sign of coming relief.

I slowly rise and with my binoculars scan the surrounding bog. Still no sign of wolves. A large insect drops from the sky and lands in a nearby pine. Soon a familiar buzz reveals the visitor's identity as a cicada. A few minutes pass and another large insect flies by and plops onto a leatherleaf. This one has a bright green body and legs — obviously a bush katydid. As I watch, it climbs around the shrub and, apparently content with its perch, begins to flutter its wings. As it vibrates these parts a raspy "ssszzzzip sszzzzip sszzzzip" can be heard. Excitedly I realize that this is the first time I have ever watched one sing. There is always some new sound, sight, or smell to bring back as a memory.

By now the sun has moved across the sky and its position, coupled with the light cloud cover, has rendered the light much better for photography. I figure I must have been here for about seven hours by now, so it is time to try to draw the wolves out. After my fourth howl a distant answer to the north can be heard. The wolf mournfully wails about the same number of times that I called but no others can be heard. I fear the pack has either moved or was never in this bog to begin with. After a 10-minute wait, I howl again, just in case the lone wolf is approaching. It answers from the same far hillside again. But this time a second adult and a group of pups joins in. These sound even farther away than the first adult, beyond the far hill. I pack up my gear and begin the trek towards them.

That trek proved to be about as fruitful as waiting in the bog. I climbed the near hillside to stay out of sight but the walking soon got tough. A large expanse of fallen balsam fir proved next to impossible to traverse. When I tried to bypass the tangle by wandering more to the east, I found nothing but more of the same. The sun was now dropping quickly in the west and I still was nowhere near the wolves. I decided to give up on this pack and struck my way back to the vehicle. Unable to find the route I took coming in, I ended up walking about twice as far as necessary and reached my vehicle just as night was falling. Because I do not carry any liquids or food on these treks, the tepid water in my truck was especially appreciated at the end of this arduous journey.

Time spent unsuccessfully waiting for wolves can never be considered wasted. There are always other animals to observe and new experiences to be enjoyed. Often a bear, moose, deer, or otter will appear unexpectedly. One of my most memorable non-wolf encounters, however, involves much smaller creatures.

I was sitting on a hillside near a rendezvous site as dawn began to break. As I waited for the wolves, the improving light allowed me to make a few notes:

All around me dew drips off the leaves, sounding almost like a light rain falling. The morning is getting brighter almost in steps, as if sheet after sheet of darkness is being lifted. Mysterious blobs now become recognizable objects, with stumps, shrubs, and rocks all taking form. Overhead, high-pitched "chits" and "checks" tell me that a flock of migrating warblers is dropping in after a night's flight. It is September and the flurry of bird activity is a prelude to cooler days ahead.

A beaver tail slap sends a surge of excitement down my spine. But time passes uneventfully except for a concentrated attack on my exposed hands and cheeks by a group of annoying sand flies. Then I hear a distant commotion. A moose splashing in the water? No, the sound is originating much closer than the distant pond. I finally realize I am hearing a rush of wings. Dozens of small birds pour in, their tiny wings whirring all around. Ruby-crowned Kinglets, Black-capped Chickadees, many warblers (I can make out Nashville, Chestnut-sided, Black-and-white, Black-throated Green, and Bay-breasted in the dimness), and a Philadelphia Vireo descend upon me. They close in, many scolding me from only inches away, some even sitting on the sticks that make up my crude blind! I now know how a small owl must feel when surrounded by one of these angry mobs. You see, this is a defensive behaviour used by small birds to drive a potential predator away. I guess they aren't sure what I am so they are giving me the once-over. I must admit I do feel like getting up and running away for all this noise is really hard on the ears!

There are many other birds above me in the trees but it is still too dark to raise my binoculars, and wolves might see the movement. So I will just sit here and enjoy the buzz of activity.

This particular rendezvous site was situated along a small stream that flowed through a partially dried-up beaver pond. An old beaver dam bordered the south end of the opening, the stream trickling unimpeded through its crumbling remains. A couple of large puddles, humble remnants of the former pond, lay near the dam. Short grass covered the rest of the open terrain where beavers once swam.

The first time I accessed this site, I walked through a forest of poplar and birch and then a dense alder thicket. After spending several uneventful hours hiding in the alders (well, not totally uneventful — I quite literally scared the s—t out of a young Great Blue Heron that wandered up the creek to within a few metres of me), I howled but got no response. I then explored the site and found plenty of wolf tracks. The old pond

I first accessed this rendezvous site through the alders at the north end of the drained beaver pond.

lay in a valley bordered by two very steep hills. As I walked along the bottom of the west-facing hill, I encountered lots of wolf sign, including several spots where wear had exposed large amounts of sand. The centre of attraction seemed to be an old sawn-off stump with a trail running underneath it. I decided to find an alternative route to this site, one that would offer me a clear view of this stump.

I walked through the water to avoid leaving too much scent around and climbed the opposite hill. Between a couple of substantial spruces I found the perfect vantage point. I pulled together all the dead limbs I could find to create a natural blind. I then crawled to the top of the hill, finding not only the easiest

This young Great Blue Heron worked its way along the creek right up to me. It was not long in departing after this photo!

route but also clearing it of any sticks that might crack underfoot when I made my predawn visit. Wolves are so in tune with their environment that one careless snap of a twig and the game is over.

After I had my approach route cleared and memorized, I found a really easy path back to the road I had parked along. I came across an old bush road covered in moss and lichens, a perfect route for sneaking in without being seen or heard. Only by returning the following morning would I find out whether all this effort was going to pay off.

Chapter 4

A RENDEZVOUS WITH WOLVES

T he next day I returned to the rendezvous site. After an arduous 4 A.M. awakening, I arrived at the old bush road well before dawn. Stepping on every patch of moss I could pick out in the darkness, I tiptoed painstakingly along the trail to the pine-covered hill that led down to the site. I weaved my way down the steep slope, appreciating my efforts of the previous day whenever my foot set down without making a sound. Finally, I reached the tangle of sticks that formed my crude blind. Behind its sparse cover, I slowly opened up my tripod and removed my long lens from its backpack. When the equipment was set up, I squatted behind it, careful not to disturb any vegetation with my feet. Folding my legs in front in a Buddha's pose, with great anticipation I began "The Wait." The following is excerpted from notes taken that unforgettable morning:

For late August it is rather warm. Although the air is laden with hazy mist this early morning, frost at this time of year is not rare. An hour has passed since I first arrived and still no sign of wolves. But a loud slap of a beaver's tail somewhere down the stream past the old dam gives me hope they are still around. Another hour passes and no other encouraging sounds have been heard. My legs

My view of the rendezvous site: after a couple of hours one starts to doubt whether wolves are really there.

are cramped and a few no-see-ums, not normally active this late in the year, are busy searing my hands and face. I offer a silent prayer that the wolves will show up before the biting insects drive me insane.

Only a minute or two after my divine request, I hear a loud crashing on the distant hillside. One, then two, finally three wolf pups appear at the bottom of the slope on the far side of the meadow. I can barely believe my eyes and my whole body shakes with excitement. The first pup walks in front of the old stump and begins digging in the soft sand. The second picks up a stick, plops down, and begins to chew on it. The third just nonchalantly walks around. I note how all three are similar in colour and pattern to

LEFT: One by one they scrambled up the slope to sleep in the cool shade of the trees.

TOP RIGHT: The old stump proved to be the focal point of this pup's interest.

BOTTOM RIGHT: The pups were obviously tired, no doubt just coming off an all-nighter.

an adult: light grey with tawny brown ears, snout, and flanks. A small amount of black appears on their backs, tails, and down the backs of their legs. The pups hang around for about five minutes then scramble back up the slope. With my binoculars I watch them lie down among the bracken ferns and go to sleep. I can see two quite well, their heads resting on their front paws.

Five or six grown-up howls rise from down the creek 15 or 20 minutes later. A rustle near the old dam attracts my attention and I see a small wolf emerge from the alders. It walks along the old dam towards me, sniffs around a bit, then steps off and saunters into the meadow. It raises its nose and checks the air

▲ Each trip to the pond usually resulted in a good long drink.

before casually walking up the slope towards the pups. It moves past the young wolves, which raise their heads but don't get up, then disappears into the trees higher up the slope.

An hour or two passes. One of the pups stands, yawns, and yelps. It ambles down the slope to one of the puddles and takes a good long drink, its pink tongue noisily lapping the water. It stretches, walks along the old beaver dam for a bit, then turns around and ventures back up the slope. Here, it plops back down and soon falls asleep. Another hour passes and no further action. The morning has now turned into a scorcher.

My eyes wander down to my camera and I check the settings for a moment or two. But when I look back up at the wolves I am

▶ After a loud "crack" beside me, the pups became quite nervous and soon vanished from their resting sites on the far slope.

▶ The reason for the pups' alarm soon became apparent.

shocked to discover they are not there. Did they spot me and take off? I decide this is hardly possible, for I have been here for at least six hours and have taken a number of photos without being detected. Just as I write this thought down, I hear a loud crack to my immediate left. My heart jumps into my throat. What is beside me? A wolf that has warned the others? A moose? A bear? It must be big to have made that loud of a noise. I glance back across at the far hill and see movement. I slowly raise my binoculars and see a pup skulking off to the right through the bracken. Then my eye catches motion down below me. Goosebumps rise on my skin when a fair-sized bear ambles out from the bottom of the slope and heads directly across the meadow to the old stump where the pups had been playing earlier. Its massive snout sniffs around the stump and then the beast climbs up the slope to where the wolves had been lying minutes ago. The bear pokes around a bit then disappears from view.

At least another hour has passed and the only sign that any bears or wolves are still around has been a short series of adult wolf howls which came from way down the creek past the old beaver dam. Another hour or so goes by, then I hear the adult and all three pups howling from the same general direction.

By this time it was well past noon and the sun was beating down with ferocious intensity. A strong, hot breeze had also come up. Thinking that the wolves will probably not return until much later in the day, I decided to leave to get some relief from the heat. I cautiously made my way out, returning about three hours later for the late shift. I soon regretted having taken the break.

The pups returned by late afternoon but were frightened off once again, quite possibly by the same bear.

As I work my way through the pines on my return trip to the blind, a couple of loud yelps announce that the pups are back! Through the trees I see the meadow and two of the pups. One is lying near the stump and the other is standing belly deep in one of the ponds casting a perfect reflection in the water. I silently curse myself for not staying. The pup in the water takes a drink, then casually saunters out of the pond. It strolls to the north end of the meadow and disappears around a bend. Again, I silently chastise myself for missing a dramatic picture. Through my camera lens I watch the other pup still sleeping by the stump and take a picture of it. Several minutes pass and then the first pup comes bounding back into view. It lopes towards the one lying down, no doubt to play, I think. But it races right past and dashes up the hill. Its sibling, awakened by the playmate's arrival, jumps up and nervously sniffs the air. Then it, too, bounds up the slope and out of sight.

I wonder if the bear has returned and scared them off. An hour or so passes and still no sign of the pups. As dusk begins to descend, I hear the distant whack of a beaver's tail. A few seconds later, an eerie scream and an ominous thrashing erupt from the distant alders well beyond the old dam. After a short silence two soft howls rise from the same location and then the yips of a pup. I wait another half an hour but see nothing. The light is almost gone so I pack up my gear. As I slowly make my way out in the darkness, my mind is alive with images of the unseen drama that has just transpired.

The pups at this rendezvous site spent considerably more time lying around and resting than being active. This pattern of sleeping for several hours then rising for a few minutes to play and drink is one that I have seen repeated at several other rendezvous sites. No doubt because most of their activity is at night, they rest much of the day.

Along the Oxtongue

The use of rendezvous sites continues right through late summer and into late fall. The following day-long observations were made in October 1996:

▲ The Oxtongue River is a beautiful waterway to canoe.

It is October 16 and the day is starting off warm and cloudy. But there is no wind — a critical factor when looking for wolves. A pack has been heard along the Oxtongue River, so I head down there. Wolves regularly frequent this river because it supports a high beaver population and the numerous grassy meadows that line the shoreline offer perfect rendezvous sites.

I howl from the highway, which parallels much of the river. Eventually at least two pups respond. A clearly defined moose trail leads off in the general direction of the wolves so I start along it. The tapestry of fallen leaves covering much of this trail offers nothing more than visual splendour. With every step I take, the dry leaves noisily crack and crunch underfoot.

The trail crosses over a mucky spot, which I know will cause problems. And it soon does, sucking down my boots until the open tops are in danger of being swallowed by the mud. Each step is a struggle not only to soften the sucking sounds but also to keep my boots on. Drier ground finally, and the walking becomes easier. Eventually, I reach a small opening from which I hear an adult wolf howl not far ahead. Two pups also add their voices to its song. Between the wolves and my clearing lies a thick tangle of young balsam fir. Behind this I can see a large opening where the wolves are probably located. After scrutiny from several angles, it seems the barrier of firs is almost impenetrable and will likely prevent me from approaching any closer without being heard. I abandon my route in favour of an approach by water.

I drive about a kilometre down the road to a parking lot that offers easy access to the river. Quickly, I load my canoe and launch it into the current. I bring along some rain gear for the cloud cover hasn't lifted any since dawn.

As I paddle against the brisk current, multitudes of birds flush from the riverbanks. I count 16 robins in one flock and at least 40 grackles in another, the latter squeaking away like a bunch of rusty hinges. Dozens more of these and other birds, including a few Rusty Blackbirds, continue to fly from the wild raisins and highbush cranberries in which they had been feasting. My canoe passes over a bed of marestail gracefully swaying in the current and I stick my hand in the water to feel their caress. Although the fall has been warm, the water soon chills my hand and I quickly return to paddling.

The river is full of curves and bends, but an examination of the aerial photo I brought along fails to reveal my exact location relative to the rendezvous site. I am forced to howl to get a fix on the wolves. An adult answers from a fair piece ahead so I know I haven't gone far enough. After more paddling, I hear another howl, but this one is coming from a very different direction — from the south, not the east. It also sounds quite different. When I hear it a second and then a third time, its human quality becomes quite apparent. So this is what a wolf hears when we howl, I chuckle to myself! To my delight, the real wolves, one adult and at least two pups, begin to howl from not far ahead. I quicken my strokes and the canoe surges forward. After navigating a couple more bends I figure I must be close and stop paddling and let the canoe silently drift. A Boreal Chickadee wheezes out a greeting from a skinny balsam fir. My heart jumps when an explosion of crashing and snarling breaks out to my immediate right. A whir of wings and a startled Ruffed Grouse flies up and lands on top of an alder. The grouse's tail flicks as it scolds the playful pups, whose wild antics have flushed it from below.

I can't see the wolves because of the alders but the cocked head of the grouse tells me that they must be just below it. Suddenly I feel terribly exposed and realize that I could be spotted at any second. With some urgency in my stroke, I try to silently move past the hidden animals and round the next bend in the river. But before I reach cover, there is more crashing quite close by and I am forced to freeze. I stop just as a pup comes running through the alders a mere six metres from my side. Fortunately, it does not see me and continues along the edge of the river. Knowing that there is no way I can advance without being seen, I desperately begin to backpaddle. More crashing and a second pup comes trotting through the alders. Again I freeze. It, too, fails to spot me and heads back into the alders, working its way towards a large opening to the north. Then more noise and I spot a third pup moving through the shrubs. I work my paddle in a backward J-stroke, never lifting it from the water to avoid making any noise.

After what seems an eternity, I succeed in backing the canoe into a little eddy along the far shore, well out of the wolves' view. I pull the canoe up on the muddy edge of this backwater and grab my gear. A beaver trail takes me over a small rise of land and, fortuitously, right back to the river at a point exactly opposite the wolves. I methodically make my way down to the riverbank, but I am worried about being discovered as long grasses noisily clutch at my tripod and pantlegs. The descent is further hindered by crispy alder leaves, which snap and crackle like Rice Crispies underfoot. Stepping around these obstacles is not easy because of slippery mud, but I eventually reach the river's edge and settle in among the leaning alders.

I sit motionless for at least 10 minutes before tending to my surroundings. A few alder branches hanging in front of my camera lens are slowly bent out of the way. With extreme care, loose sticks are placed in the branches around me, creating a crude blind of sorts. To keep my butt at least semi-dry, I place under it a chunk of wood left behind by the higher spring waters. At last I feel sufficiently hidden.

The view I have of the far shore is limited but includes two little points of mud that project out from either side of a small inlet. If a wolf obliges and comes down to drink I will have a perfect view. But apart from a single crash that I heard on the far side a while ago, there is no evidence of the wolves. Perhaps they are having a snooze, likely under the scattered spruces that stand behind the alders.

The clouds have dissipated and the sun now beams down with strong conviction. First my coat, then my heavy shirt comes off. Small red dragonflies

▼ Yellow-legged Meadowhawks kept me company while I waited for the wolves to emerge from the shoreline alders.

start to fly all around, many paired up in tandem with the brown and green females. A red male lands nearby and I strain to see its leg colour. Pale legs reveal it to be a yellow-legged meadowhawk. A sudden crash diverts my attention back to the far shore. A chipmunk scolds and I wonder if my ears have exaggerated the sounds of its scampering. The loud snap of a stick soon dispels that notion. The noise continues to draw nearer, but before the animal appears I hear growling and then yelps of submission. I breathe a sigh of relief. The pups are still here and are just across from my vantage point!

I hear a bit more noise that sounds like play and then all becomes quiet again. I can picture the pups lying by the base of those spindly black spruces that rise just behind the alders.

The wind is picking up and leaves begin to tumble down from the sky, landing and spinning on the water like little sailboats. Hours pass and nothing but wind and dozens of meadowhawks are moving. During this lull I add bits of dead fern and spirea to my hiding spot. Finally I hear a bark, then an animal running from somewhere across the river. But only the alders and water are visible. Then I hear a lapping sound to my right. I look over and see a pup at the water's edge, contentedly drinking away. Damn — too many alder branches in the way to get a clear shot. So I sit and watch. The pup quenches its thirst, then climbs back up the steep slope, slipping partway up. As soon as it disappears over the top of the bank, I hear a strong yelp. Sounds like it was ambushed by one of its siblings.

Silence sets back in. The sun has moved far to my right and I now sit in the shade of several tall spruce. The temperature quickly drops, and one by one the pieces of shed clothing are put back on. The far side of the river is still in good light but the wolves have yet to appear here. I wonder if they are still sleeping or if they have moved farther down the river. It is oh so tempting to howl and find out where they are, but I decide to wait. Earlier the sky had been totally clear but now a few puffy clouds ride the upper air currents and steadily drift southeast. No doubt it will be a cooler day tomorrow.

Blue Jays scream from a group of firs and a Pileated Woodpecker that had earlier been beating up a dead spruce calls its loud stutter. I wonder whether the birds have spotted a wolf or a small owl hidden away waiting for dark to fall. The answer remains a mystery for the birds fall silent as the sun sinks lower in the western sky. Shadows come out from their daytime retreats and begin to stretch across the river.

I decide it is time to try to draw a wolf out into my field of view before the sun vanishes for the day. I howl three singles but nothing answers. Have they gone? I try squealing on my fingers to imitate an injured animal. This results in some rustling in the bushes, then movement, and three heads poke through the alders across from me. I am tempted to take a photograph but decide to wait until the wolves come out. This is a mistake, for one begins to stare right at me. I don't move a muscle yet the pup gets wise to me and gives a short bark before disappearing into the alders. I howl and one begins to whine, almost breaking into a howl. I squeak some more and I hear the threesome dashing around in the alders. Then a loud, deep bark announces that an adult has also arrived. The barks become more frequent and aggressive. I know the game is up, so I just sit quietly to see what will transpire. One by one, all three pups bound towards the opening behind the alders to the east. The adult barks a few more times, as if telling me my presence is not appreciated. Several minutes pass and I howl. The adult barks back from some distance away. I pack up my gear and, leg muscles paralyzed and bottom numbed by the long sit, painfully stumble up the trail to my canoe. I throw the load in and begin the long paddle back with the sun resting just above the horizon. As I navigate another oxbow, the adult wolf barks again from just behind, obviously making sure that I am leaving.

I arrived back at my starting point well after sundown and lifted the canoe onto the truck before wandering over to the river to howl for the wolves. A French-speaking couple who dropped by were invited to join me to listen to *les loups*. We stood on a foot bridge over the river and faced the east, admiring the final glow of the evening sky. My howl echoed down the river to the wolves, which answered back in full chorus. It appeared the full pack had reunited as not one but three adults howled back with the pups. The French couple asked in very broken English whether those strange sounds were made by other people. I replied in very broken French that, no, they were not. We were all hearing the genuine voice of the wild!

Whenever possible, I return to a rendezvous site a day later and howl to see if the animals are still present. In this case I was unable to do so; Gord, a fellow working at the Visitor Centre, did the check for me. To my great relief, the pack was there the following night when he howled from the highway.

There is always a fear that a visit to a rendezvous site might disturb the wolves and force them to leave. That is why I so rarely visit rendezvous sites, and when I do, take such care in accessing them. That is also why I usually return to satisfy myself that I have not disturbed them. If I inadvertently disturb an animal, I feel that I have done it a great injustice. Nothing is more gratifying than spending a day with wolves and knowing my presence has not affected them.

A Wolf Near Sunday Creek

While several of my trips into rendezvous sites have provided hours of privileged observation, on some occasions, the journey yielded only a brief encounter with an adult or a pup. Such was the case when I visited a site along Sunday Creek. It was mid-September and I had worked my way along a moose trail towards a suspected rendezvous site. My notes from this day tell the story:

> The well-worn moose trail has finally led me through the firs and spruce to the opening I had seen on the aerial photograph last night. As suspected, it is an old beaver pond gone dry, with a scattering of grasses and sedges now replacing most of the water. All through the mud a forest of fallen trees lies as if sleeping. At the east end I see a large rock between a white spruce and a balsam fir — an ideal spot to hide. Like a tightrope walker gripping a balance stick, I hold out my tripod as I precariously walk from log to log. I figure if the wolves are still here, then my odds of not scaring them off are better if I leave my scent trail in the middle of the pond instead of around its edges.

▼ A large rock outcrop covered in spruce and fir offered me a perfect vantage point of the suspected rendezvous site near Sunday Creek.

I reach my lofty perch and settle in behind the spruce. What a perfect hiding spot: the sun will rise behind me and I have a clear view of the pond ahead. An hour passes and the mist begins to burn off. During the wait a few birds begin to stir. A Lincoln's Sparrow, soon to depart for warmer haunts, flits up beside me and chips its surprise. The squeaky call of a Black-backed Woodpecker precedes a series of slow, heavy pecks. No doubt looking for bark beetles on some dead spruce. I call and immediately a deep, hoarse howl answers me from the south. The wolf howls twice and then all is still. As I wait for the animal to approach, I hear a crack of wood, then soft footfalls off to my right. Hair brushes against twigs and I see a small wolf emerging from the trees. It pauses for a minute, looking out over the pond in the direction from which the other wolf had howled. It moves towards me and passes on the far side of the spruce in which I am partially hidden, its grey coat catching on branches only metres from me. I pray it doesn't smell or see me. The wolf passes right by. From just behind me I hear its nails clicking on rock and its footpads compressing moss. Then nothing. I figure it has gone towards the wolf that had answered my howls, so I wait to see if any others appear.

About half an hour passes and only a pair of White-winged Crossbills and a curious Gray Jay visit me. I howl again. I almost jump off my rock when a loud howl erupts right behind me! The wolf hadn't gone very far at all. I hear it running towards me and I figure the game will soon be over. But then I see movement to my left. There, just on the far side of the balsam fir beside me, is the wolf. It is looking straight down the pond in the direction I had thrown my voice. It walks out on a log about 12 metres away, stops, and howls. There is my dream shot, a wolf standing in side profile in plain view, howling away! But my camera is pointing straight down the pond. The only way I can photograph the wolf

After watching the wolf howl from half this distance away, I finally had a reasonable view of it through the camera lens. To my surprise, the mist was due to condensation on the lens and not early morning fog!

After wiping off the lens with my shirt, I was able to get a much clearer picture of the wolf.

is to grab my tripod and step in front of the balsam fir, but this will surely scare off the animal. So I sit tight and through the corner of my eye relish a sight that so few people have enjoyed.

After it finishes howling, the wolf walks off the log and wanders along the edge of the pond. Fortunately, it is walking away from me so I grab the tripod and move it past the fir. I set it quietly down, breathing a silent sigh of relief that the wolf did not see this. I aim the lens at the wolf and take a shot. Funny, it still looks quite misty through the lens. A quick glance above the camera tells me that there is no mist and my lens is fogged! I swing the lens towards me and wipe off the misty coating with my shirt. The wolf is still walking along, paying no heed. But it has moved some distance so

I know that if I want to photograph it howling, the time is now or never. I howl and the wolf stops. I have a wonderful view in my lens, the creature standing in the rushes at the pond's edge in front of a backdrop of dead spruce boughs. It looks towards me but does not howl. I take one shot and wait. It hears the shutter click but does not see me. It turns away for a moment, so I swing the lens around and clean off the film of water once more. I quickly focus on the wolf again. It turns and I take two more shots while howling softly. Please howl back, I silently plead. But it does not, instead staring intently until it finally keys in on me. It barks, turns, and strolls into the spruces. I howl again but no response. A few minutes pass and I hear the wolf howl from some distance to the southwest. Not wishing to disturb it any more, I pack up and leave.

I returned that night and howled from the highway. The pack including several pups howled back from roughly the same location as they had several nights earlier. I realize that I had just not worked my way in far enough that morning. But I felt I had my chance with this pack and made no further effort to work them.

Wolves on the Move

Wolves will change rendezvous sites throughout the summer if they are disturbed by humans or bears. But I am certain that they move for other reasons as well, such as to get closer to a better supply of food.

One August night I had the good fortune to come across a pack on the move. It was approaching midnight when I heard an entire pack spontaneously howl not far off the road. Up until that night the same pack had been located not far from Brewer Lake. They were now on the move — several adults and a handful of pups — all heading east from that lake. I met them not far from West Smith Lake. As they ran along the edge of a waterway that paralleled the highway, I could hear their feet splashing in the water. Every few minutes an adult would howl, soon enticing the rest of the pack to join in. The constant racket of the entire group gave me the impression that the howling was being used to ensure none of the pups wandered astray during the journey.

I tried to keep ahead of the pack, parking on the shoulder and waiting for the wolves to draw near before moving ahead again. Over the three hours spent tracking, the pack moved only about five kilometres. Mind you, this was measured in highway mileage; in wolf mileage, the pack probably travelled at least half that distance again, for the creek twisted and turned and veered away from the highway at one point. The wolves ended up just south of the East Gate late that night and were still there when I checked again at dawn. Their stay was brief, however. The next night the pack was gone, having moved to an unknown location.

Fortunately, visitors to Algonquin Park can enjoy wolves without expending all this effort and in less intrusive ways. Each year thousands of people experience these magnificent animals by taking part in organized night outings. While you do not actually walk into a rendezvous site, the encounter is almost as dramatic. Listening to the wild music of wolves echoing through the night stirs the soul like no other sound on the planet.

 Venturing out after the sun goes down is only part of the attraction of a Public Howl.

Chapter 5

THE HOWLS OF AUGUST

T wo thousand strong stand in the dark, fending off the night chill as they anxiously wait for the concert to begin. Tonight, though, the group this crowd has come to hear is of a much wilder nature than the norm. This crisp evening it is the music of wolves that has attracted the crowd to one of Algonquin's celebrated Public Wolf Howls.

Held only in late summer, Public Wolf Howls are highly acclaimed interpretive events in which park visitors venture out to hear wild wolves howl at night. For the uninitiated, any event with such a pedestrian title and boasting an average attendance of well over 1,000 participants might have little appeal. But one excursion and almost all newcomers become avid fans of the Howl.

Public Wolf Howls date back to August 17, 1963. "The night we go out howling for wolves" was how the inaugural excursion was modestly billed in that year's August 14 issue of the park newsletter, *The Raven*. The invitation's author, seasonal park naturalist Russ Rutter, anticipated 20 cars at most, certainly not the 200 or so that showed up for the event. This unexpected turnout resulted in "the biggest traffic jam ever witnessed in Algonquin Park."

The crowd of about 650 gathered at the Two Rivers Picnic Area, where Department of Lands and Forests biologist George

Kolenosky first gave a brief talk on wolves. When they ventured out, the organizers hoped that either taped recordings or human imitations of wolf howls would trigger a response from any eavesdropping wolves. Both methods had proven highly successful during the wolf research program initiated in Algonquin in 1958 (and completed in 1965). To the delight of all those present on this initial outing, the wolves responded rather well.

The first Public Wolf Howl was a significant event, of far greater importance than the auditory gratification of the crowd on hand that night. A new and compelling vehicle to interpret the value of Algonquin wolves had just been launched.

Since that first effort, well-attended even by today's standards, to the time of writing, 77 Public Wolf Howls with a total participation just shy of 100,000 have been held. The success rate is equally impressive, with wolves heard on 73 percent of all howls!

The success of the Public Wolf Howls depends on two features of wolf biology: wolves respond as readily to human imitations as they do to howls of other wolves; and wolf packs remain at rendezvous sites for extended periods of time in late summer. In advance of a Public Wolf Howl, which is usually held on a Thursday in August, summer staff scout for wolves on the two nights prior to the anticipated event. If wolves are present at a rendezvous site on a Wednesday evening, participants are brought within earshot of the pack the next day. If wolves are not located or have vanished by the Wednesday night, a regular interpretive program is offered in place of the Howl.

The Pog Lake
Outdoor Theatre

Every Public Wolf Howl is a memorable event — and not just for
the howls. Participants gather at the Pog Lake Outdoor Theatre,
where they are greeted by a small legion of flashlight-bearing,
reflector-vested park staff who guide them through the maze of

▲ LEFT ABOVE: Most of the naturalists are responsible
for parking the hundreds of cars that arrive at the
Pog Lake Outdoor Theatre.

LEFT BELOW: The evening is launched by Dan
Strickland welcoming the masses to the Howl.

RIGHT: Well before the theatre program begins, the
800 seats are taken.

parking pods. As the cars steadily flow in, a dazzling light show develops. Shafts of light from their headlights probe the rising cloud of dust and intersect the golden arcs blazed by the vigorously waved parking batons. Like ants heading off to a picnic, the occupants of the parked vehicles stream down to the amphitheatre for the prehowl show. The first 800 to arrive, some an hour before the official starting time, are rewarded with a seat on the wooden benches. The next one to two thousand have to stand for the presentation.

After welcoming the highly energized crowd to the Howl, Dan Strickland, Chief Park Naturalist since the late 1960s, hands over the microphone to Ron Tozer, recently retired Park Naturalist, who presents a slide talk on wolves and wolf howling. His highly entertaining talk culminates in the playing of recorded wolf howls, and a thunderous round of applause demonstrates the audience's appreciation. The microphone is returned to Dan, who outlines the procedure for getting to the howling site. Near the end of Dan's instructions, Ron and the second "howler" are brought onstage to demonstrate the vocal offerings that will be used to incite the wolves. After Dan's closing remarks, like three pied pipers he, Ron, and the second howler lead the excited masses back to the parking lot.

At the howling site, cars line both sides of the road for almost two kilometres.

Driving to the Howling Site

Hundreds of cars leave the amphitheatre and adjacent parking areas and move down the highway in a near-endless convoy. Staff make sure that vehicles enter the procession in the same controlled manner in which they had been parked. Park vehicles located at both ends and in the middle of the cavalcade, which stretches for many kilometres along the highway, maintain order during the exodus to the wolf location. A count of the vehicles as they entered the parking lot makes it possible for Dan to insert vehicles into the middle of the exiting line, functionally cutting it into two halves. When the first half has passed the howling location, it is turned around and led back against the flow of the second half. By inserting the total number of vehicles into an ingenious mathematical formula, Dan determines precisely where the lead car in each line must stop so that both lines are centered at the howling location. More often than not, the lead car in one line and the last car in the second line end up virtually across the road from one another. To prevent overly eager participants from driving directly to the howling site and throwing the entire operation into chaos, the location is kept secret until the end of the theatre program. Wardens patrol the site as well to keep it clear of vehicles.

Viewed from a vantage point on any of the hills along the highway, the procession is quite a splendid spectacle. Head- and tail-lights blend into sinuous streams of white and red that twist

▲ Participants stand outside their vehicles waiting eagerly for the howls to begin.

and bend through the dark night. When the cars finally roll to a halt and the occupants bail out, the repetitive flashing on and off of interior lights is not unlike a major convention of fireflies.

The Howl

With thousands of participants lining the road, one might think it would be impossible to hear the wolves above the incessant chatter and shuffling of feet. Remarkably, the excited crowd stands in near silence, and waits for the howls to begin. When the signal is finally given, Ron Tozer lets loose a powerful howl. A kilometre away, the most distant participants hear his call and everyone excitedly perks up, straining to hear a response. Anxious seconds pass. If wolves do not answer, a second howl is given, and a third if necessary. Both howlers deliver a series of howls if wolves have failed to reply, but "group howls" are not usually needed. On most outings wolves respond by Ron's third howl.

A typical response consists of the wild yips and yaps of several pups and the longer, deeper howls of a couple of adults. If the night is calm and cool (as is typical of August) and the wolves are not too far away, every participant is able to hear the howls. Despite being in the presence of at least a thousand others, for each the experience is profoundly personal.

A second round of howling takes place after a 15-minute wait. During this interval, any highway traffic held back is allowed to continue on its way. (It must be rather strange for someone driving through the "wilderness" to come upon a seemingly endless line of parked cars, with thousands of people standing beside them.)

After the second attempt — and if wolves have been heard — the ecstatic crowd responds with a deafening round of applause before scrambling back into their cars. The participants leave with lasting memories. As for the wolves, they seem to tolerate the brief intrusion quite well. A wolf pack often remains at a Howl site, making it possible to hold additional Public Howls there.

Overly enthusiastic participants have been known to return

later on the night of a Howl or on succeeding nights and howl for the wolves. Unfortunately, these efforts can become nothing short of harassment, especially if the wolves are howled at for hours on end. If you take part in a Public Howl, I recommend you try to howl up your own wolves at a different location.

Scouting Before the Howl

During my tenure as a seasonal interpretive naturalist in Algonquin, I was involved in at least 30 Public Wolf Howls. Duties included scouting for wolves, parking cars, directing traffic, and acting as the second howler.

Scouting for wolves on an Algonquin night was always more of an adventure than work. Before setting off, we filled the truck with flashlights, extra clothing, music tapes, pop, and copious quantities of cookies and other snacks. The latter items provided the energy needed to keep us alert between howling sites (which are usually separated by at least several kilometres).

The four of us would split into two teams, with each team covering half of the highway corridor. Regardless of which part of the park a team covered, at any time you could expect to have a fox or moose dash across the road in front of the vehicle. As we drove, we looked for eyeshine along the sides of the road. Since an animal's eyes reflect a specific colour of light, it is not too difficult to ascertain the species by the colour of the eyeshine: green for fox (although the eyeshine of the rarely seen fisher is also this colour); white for deer or moose; and a startling ruby red for Whip-poor-wills. When two animals share the same colour, the height of the eyeshine above the ground helps to pinpoint the species.

Void of the glow of man-made lights, the nights in Algonquin are deliciously dark. The immensity of the night would swallow us up as soon as we stepped out of the vehicle and we would stand in silence, completely absorbed by the star-drenched spectacle overhead. A shooting star burning its way across the heavens or the contorted dance of the colourful Aurora would pull our thoughts far away from wolves. But only for a moment, as strange night sounds would bring us back to Earth.

Today, scouting for wolves today has retained much of its aura, although some things have changed considerably since the early 1970s. Twenty-five years ago, it was possible to scout the highway corridor with your partner in near solitude. Since then, highway use has increased so much that you often have to wait 10 or 15 minutes for enough of a break in the traffic noise to start the howls. On particularly busy nights this aggravation persists well toward midnight.

A wolf pack found on the first night's scouting trip has to be present on the Wednesday night before being considered usable for the Howl. On the second evening Dan Strickland shows up to case the situation. He determines where the "howlers" should be located by listening to the responses from several different locations and examining the lay of the land. If the terrain offers good listening from all points along the highway, the queues of cars are centred as close to the pack as possible; the presence of hills dictate a shift in the lines in one direction. On this final scouting expedition no one is permitted to return to the staffhouse for a well-deserved rest until the car positioning has been nailed down.

The Day of the Howl

Dan Strickland, the grand maestro of the Howls, goes over the operational details at a prehowl meeting.

The day of a Public Wolf Howl is never business as usual. Museum phone lines are jammed with inquiries, even though notices of the event are posted around the park. People from as far away as Toronto and even Windsor are interested in knowing when and where a Howl will take place.

Public Wolf Howl days take their toll on every member of the naturalist staff, including Dan. On these days he is focused on the business at hand, and becomes predictably listless and irritable. Considering the organizational logistics, this is not surprising. Preparations involve assigning roles to the staff working that night, procuring volunteers and equipment, planning for the movement of the crowd to and from the howling location, controlling through-traffic on the highway, and ensuring that the particular requirements of media crews covering the Howl are met. Every detail has to be painstakingly mapped out.

Later that day staff members involved in the Howl are given their instructions. Everyone is assigned a role, specific equipment, and a spot in a vehicle. That evening, staff attend a strategy meeting at the naturalists' staffhouse, and woe to anyone who arrives late! Dan clearly and concisely goes over all the instructions, using flip charts to clarify each person's responsibilities. With instructions completed and equipment distributed, the crew sets off for the Outdoor Theatre.

The first responsibility of the summer naturalists is to park the vehicles arriving at the Theatre. This job is actually exciting — and helps to get the adrenaline flowing. An endless string of cars surges by you, their tires crunching on gravel and their light beams pirouetting through clouds of dust. As the cars pass, they pull cold air behind them, bringing goose bumps to your skin.

At the parking lot, one attendant counts the cars and relays the final tally to Dan for use in his formula. Another directs the incoming cars to different pods where other attendants guide them into their parking spots. Usually this operation runs smoothly, but occasionally little glitches crop up: a driver who doesn't speak English or can't back up into the parking spot; on rare occasions a car will run out of gas or break down.

My most memorable parking lot incident took place in August 1972 on one of my first Public Wolf Howls. A large station wagon (from Indiana I believe) had entered my pod. As I was finishing my blurb about backing the car into the parking space, a woman in the back seat held a bundle wrapped in a blanket up to the window. She asked if I would like to see her baby, and being a friendly public servant, I felt obligated to say "yes." You can imagine my startled reaction, however, when she pulled back the blanket to display a pair of big, dark eyes set in a black, furry face. It took only a second or so for my thoughts to switch from "What an inordinately ugly baby!" to "Oh, my God! That woman is holding a bear cub in her arms!" It turned out that the group in the car had found the baby bear wandering around their campground earlier that day and had decided to adopt it as a pet. After a moment or two of panic, I notified a senior staff member about my predicament, and a conservation officer was called in. The cub was taken from the people. If it had remained in their car, it would have been the very first bear to officially attend a Public Wolf Howl!

Some assignments on Howl day are better than others. The least popular job is to hold back highway traffic. Well removed from the Howling location, you cannot see the line of parked cars or even hear wolves howl. Also, it isn't much fun to be on the receiving end of a lively diatribe uttered by some angry trucker who does not appreciate being held up for 15 minutes by a bunch of people listening for wolves. For me, a few of these "conversations" almost turned physical — and not only with truckers. How was I to know that police officers were to be treated any differently?

No matter how trivial you perceive your role to be, you are expected (quite rightly) to perform it with a high degree of professionalism. Dan does not tolerate any tomfoolery, and with his short fuse, it is best not to mess up on any detail, including radio communication. Park staff keep in touch on a Howl using both portable and vehicle-mounted radios. Only pertinent communication is allowed during the parking operation and en route to and from the howling site. During the howling itself, radios are to remain silent.

One year a somewhat impulsive young naturalist was handed the responsibility of controlling the through-traffic on the highway. The howling sequence was about to begin and all was quiet. The fellow decided that Dan should be informed of a minor problem: a car he was holding back still had its engine running. It obviously did not occur to him that those participating in the Howl a good mile away were unlikely to hear the noise. An incredibly loud message over the park's vehicle radios (which receive even when the engines are off) suddenly shattered the silence. The first message, heard by many of the 2,000 in attendance, was not the one that got the poor fellow in really hot water, however. The second transmission, the one sent after Dan's firm response to get off the radio, was what did him in. When the persistent fellow radioed the second time with the message, "There is some stupid knob here who won't turn off his engine." You could sense the steam escaping from Dan.

My big moment came on my second year of the Howls. The pride I felt at being listed as second howler culminated that evening when I was called onto the amphitheatre stage to give the howling demonstration. What an unforgettable thrill it was for this 20-year-old neophyte to perform as a professional wolf howler in front of a standing-room-only house!

I have been second howler on a number of other occasions since then. It's a straightforward job: you stand beside Ron Tozer and howl only when a group howl is needed (which is almost never). Occasionally, however, the usual sequence of events turns into an unexpected adventure.

A few years ago Ron and I had been dropped off at the howling site. The howlers have to arrive well before the first cars in the line so that the drivers are not tempted to stop beside the howlers in an effort to acquire a better listening spot. Naturally, this would disrupt the flow of traffic. Ron and I scrambled quickly off the roadside and down the steep embankment. We found a cosy hiding spot among some large rocks and settled in for the wait. It usually takes at least 15 minutes for all the traffic to come to a halt once it begins to pull off, and so we remained hidden when we heard tires crunching on the shoulder of the road. We knew we could soon make an appearance when we finally heard car doors opening and closing. But just before we did so, we heard a couple of men approaching our hiding spot, chattering away in a foreign language. The voices got louder and we soon heard their shoes scraping on the rocks above us. Our chuckles at not being discerned quickly vanished and we hurriedly shouted our presence. I am not quite sure who was more shocked: our visitors, at hearing loud voices suddenly coming out from the dark; or us, at hearing the telltale unzipping of trousers above our heads!

BONNECHERE'S PUBLIC WOLF HOWL

Although I no longer participate in the Algonquin Public
Wolf Howls, I am still involved in another Howl that takes
place in a different part of the park. Only a stone's throw away
from Basin Depot in southeastern Algonquin, Bonnechere
Provincial Park started an annual howling event in 1993, which I
have been privileged to lead. The prehowl talk is given in
Bonnechere Park, but the howl itself takes place across the road
at Basin Depot. Considerably more modest in format, the
Bonnechere Howl is held only once a year and draws a couple of
hundred people. Despite the fact that no one scouts for wolves
in advance, the Howl has been highly successful so far, with wolves
heard on two of the four outings. On both occasions, we had
pups on one side of us and at least one adult on the other. As well,
an adult howled back from very close range on the second set of
howls.

Public Wolf Howls are now offered in several other places in
North America. No matter where they are held, as interpretive
events, all are extremely important. There is no better way for
a person to develop an appreciation for any animal, including
timber wolves, than to meet them first-hand. And there is no
better way to experience wolves than to hear a pack howling
under a star-studded sky. Since the first outing in 1963,
Algonquin's Public Wolf Howls have introduced nearly 100,000

 Even when in the company of a thousand others, hearing wild wolves howl in the moonlight is an unforgettable experience.

people to these legendary creatures. Many have been children, who have brought or in time will bring their own families on one of these August evening outings. May their children's lives be equally enriched by the soul-stirring symphonies that define these extraordinary public events.

Chapter 6

IN SEARCH OF WOLVES

T he elusive timber wolf comes from a wilder era. Algonquin, with its untamed landscape, epitomizes the wild country wolves have always roamed. Here, the search for wolves takes you through lichen-choked forests and up rugged Shield outcrops, over quaking bog mats and along meandering rivers and streams.

The more time you spend in Algonquin — canoeing the quiet waters, walking little-used trails, and camping under northern skies — the more likely you are to encounter a wolf. But just being out there may not be enough. Given that wolves can quickly detect any anomalous sound, smell, or movement, you improve your odds significantly by learning to think and act like a wolf. Travel alone or in small groups; walk slowly and silently, preferably in the early hours of the morning or at the end of the day; wear drab-coloured clothing; and avoid soap and shampoo.

It also helps to hear and see like a wolf. Be conscious of every sound and movement around you; isolate every rustle, scratch, and footstep from the background noise of wind and water; and distinguish every flit of an ear and twist of a head from the trembling of breeze-kissed leaves.

Because wolves respond well to human imitations of their howls, you can make direct contact by vocalizing like one of

▲ By the end of summer, puppy voices begin to change
and short howls are added to their vocabulary.

them. Few moments are as thrilling as when the howls of an
entire pack shatter the silence in response to your calls. But
don't think you need a particularly superior howl to raise
wolves. Sounds as discordant as a blaring trumpet and a crying
baby have been reputed to cause wolves to respond.

Still, it is best to emulate the real thing as closely as
possible. Unlike the howls given by many novices, a wolf's
trademark song does not start off with a series of barks. This
type of call belongs to the coyote, the first cousin of the wolf. In
general, a good imitation of a howl is a loud offering released in
one continuous breath. The howl should come from deep in the

WHY WOLVES HOWL

Although we do not and probably will never fully understand the language of wolves, we do know that their howls communicate a number of different messages.

Wolves are territorial animals and their howls help to announce and define territory boundaries. Within a pack, howls allow members to communicate with each other. And it seems that howling also serves to maintain the social bond that keeps a pack together. Just like participants in a campfire singalong, wolves taking part in a pack group howl seem to be enjoying themselves.

Contrary to popular belief, wovles do not howl at the moon nor do they howl while they are on the chase. However, wolves do howl in response to a strange wolf's howl, which is why they so readily respond to our imitations.

When a human howls like a wolf, the chances of a response do not depend on the person's age or sex. Wolf voices vary just like ours, and wolves do not seem to discriminate between different howlers. I have heard wolves answer back as readily to a three year old child as they did to a man in his eighties.

throat and, through the diaphragm's influence, rise to a peak and then fall toward the end.

While the length of the howl is not critical, it is best to sustain it as long as possible. Less important are the pitch and tone, which vary almost as much in wolves as they do in humans. (I have heard wolf howls that are inspiring and those

The campsite on Fork Lake where my son Harrison proved that sometimes a high-pitched howl is better than a deeper rendition.

that sound downright awful, including one wolf whose howl cracked and broke so much with the effort that I wondered if I was hearing the howl of a heavy smoker with a bad cold.) The variation in pitch and tone allows wolves to distinguish members of their own pack from strangers, including human impersonators.

Despite the variation, adult wolves usually release a long, deep howl. Young pups, on the other hand, produce high-pitched yips and yaps, which from a distance sound not unlike the clamor of migrating geese. Their juvenile voices start to change by the end of summer, however, and short, high-pitched howls eventually become part of their vocal repertoire.

When I howl for wolves, I use the time-tested procedure refined by Algonquin's interpretive staff. I howl once, then listen for a response. If none comes after 20 or 30 seconds, I howl again. From personal experience I have found that if wolves are going to respond, they will usually do so after this second offering. It is almost as if the first howl just gets their attention. But wolves are not always that predictable and will sometimes answer back after the first or third howl. If three single howls fail to arouse a wolf, occasionally a "group howl" works. By howling together, two or more people can create the illusion that a pack of wolves is present. To avoid sounding like one giant wolf, each participant throws out three or four howls that only slightly overlap those of the other howlers. When I am alone, which is the norm, I am still able to muster up a "group" howl by howling about a dozen times in rapid succession and alternating the pitch of each howl.

If wolves do not respond by the third group howl, it is wise to move to another site. A lack of response, however, does not necessarily mean that wolves were not within earshot. On several occasions, regardless of how many times I howled, I failed to get a response from wolves that I knew were present.

Over the years I have found that various pitches of howls can elicit different responses from wolves. While a standard howl works well in most situations, if pups are quite close by, short, higher-pitched howls seem to draw better responses. A short bark or two added to a deep, long howl often elicits aggressive responses from one of the dominant adults that

Often one is best alerted to the presence of wolves by their signs.

Be sure to give a howl if you encounter fresh scats.

control the pack (the pair is known in biological circles as the alpha pair). A deep howl probably suggests a more powerful intruder; a higher-pitched howl a smaller, more subordinate animal, which is less of a threat and therefore requires a less drastic response. (By the way, contrary to what might be a popular assumption, male wolves do not appear to have deeper howls than females. I have met deep-voiced wolves that I thought must be males prove me wrong when I saw them urinate in a squat position.)

The effects of differing pitches of howls was made quite apparent during a summer canoe trip. A number of years ago, I was camping with my family on Fork Lake, which is a short paddle from Highway 60 south along Sunday Creek. The first morning of our stay I slipped out of the tent at about 5:30 and greeted the day with several howls. Apart from a wonderful echo from the mist-shrouded hills surrounding the small lake, the only response I got was the rustling of sleeping bags. About 15 minutes later, my son Harrison, who was six at the time, came stumbling out of the tent. Emulating his dad, he gave a couple of howls, which were obviously inferior to mine, being shorter and much higher-pitched. Needless to say, an entire pack of wolves on the far shore erupted in song! To this day, Harrison delights in informing those who admire my wolf impersonations that his howls are even better. Why do children have such good memories?

When and Where to Howl

Wolves are most vocal during the period they are using rendezvous sites, but you needn't wait for summer to try out your howls. Although perhaps not quite as readily, wolves will answer back at other times of the year.

As for the hour of the day, there are several advantages to howling for wolves after the sun goes down. Wolves are more vocal at night, the cool air carries sound much better, and most songbirds and other animals are quiet by the end of the day. Also absent is the annoying rustle of leaves, the wind being typically calm at night. Under the rich ambience of the night,

WOLF RESEARCH IN ALGONQUIN

During my wanderings deep into Algonquin, I would often cross paths with wolf researchers. These were either graduate students working on their Masters or Doctorate degrees under Dr. John Theberge of the University of Waterloo, and their assistants, or the "wolf man," Theberge himself, and his equally dedicated wife, Mary. Most times I would run into them while travelling obscure logging roads or camping on the shores of remote lakes. No matter where they took place, I always relished these chance meetings. Regardless if they were brief crossings or shared campfires, we would inevitably talk about unusual birds or mammals we had encountered, and, of course, swap stories about wolves.

Although our association was mostly personal, I once helped man a wolf trap line near Rock Lake. Here, a road-killed White-tailed deer was being used to lure the wolves in to the leg-hold traps. The month was July and the mercury rose to new heights daily, as did the stench from the bait. Although I never did catch a wolf during my short research stint, a Turkey Vulture ended up paying the price for visiting the carcass.

Over the years, vultures were not the only animals to wander into the researchers' traps. Foxes were the most regular non-target creatures but even skunks appeared on occasion. One early June day I was conducting a hawk survey near Achray on Grand Lake when the distinctive Waterloo wolf van appeared with the ever-present bags of wolf scats hanging from the side mirrors. I knew something was up when I could make out Graham Forbes, the driver, hanging out the open windows. Sure enough, while attempting to release a skunk from a trap, Graham received a face full of spray when one of the girls accompanying him (I believe it was Lee, now his wife) let her foot slip off the skunk's tail!

I have nothing but respect for the tenacity of the researchers. While you might think the study of wolves to be a euphoric, even romantic pasttime, it is really a difficult job. Near-sleepless nights out searching for wolves, pre-dawn rises to check the traps, countless kilometres walked in unforgiving terrain, and meals well below the level of soup kitchen fare were par for the course. And for most of the season there were the biting flies. Black flies started off the season. When these began to wane mosquitoes took over. Even the heat of mid-summer failed to provide relief from the blood-letters, for then deer flies joined the attack. I don't know how many times I barely recognized a familiar and once-pretty face because it was obscured by a mask of bleeding sores.

But the researchers and their assistants endured and persisted. For them, locating wolf packs was the easy part of the job. The difficult part was capturing their members to equip them with radio transmitters. But once they succeeded, the data acquired by following a "collared" wolf around provided great insight into its movements both inside and outside Algonquin, as well as into the perils faced by these elusive animals

with a sky dotted with a thousand points of light, a wolf's howl pulls your emotions to a new high as it rises and falls in the dark.

Following a chorus of song, wolves are usually reluctant to howl again until some time has passed. Reported to last up to 20

LEFT ABOVE: Graham Forbes, who did his doctorate on Algonquin wolves, gently holds a trapped wolf with a forked stick while the animal is tranquillized.

RIGHT ABOVE: Once researchers locate wolves, they carefully set leg-hold traps for them.

RIGHT BELOW: After all measurements are recorded (here, by Cam Roberts), a leather collar with a transmitter is put around the animal's neck.

LEFT BELOW: Once drugged, the wolf is weighed with expensive scientific instruments.

minutes, I have never experienced this silence to go beyond several minutes. In fact, one group of pups that I met one late August day while scouting near Wolf Howl Pond couldn't wait to answer.

Although it was close to noon, generally the poorest time of day for hearing wolves, I thought I would howl just for something to do. I must admit I was rather surprised when a group of pups responded from the north. While they were howling, I decided to try a little experiment to see how long it took before they would howl a second time. My plan was to howl as soon as they stopped, and then every 30 seconds after that, until they responded. The pups howled back the moment my next howl died, and just as their response faded, I howled again. They responded in this fashion 11 consecutive times before refusing to answer any more.

When searching for wolves, try howling from hilltops and beside creek valleys. These are ideal locations because your calls and the wolves' responses carry farther. Also, when you are walking trails or old roads, keep an eye out for fresh tracks and droppings, known as scats. These will often lead you right to wolves. Even when driving, be on the lookout for wolf sign. Particularly good roads for sign are Basin Depot, Sand Lake, Rock Lake, and Opeongo Lake. In summer, watch for groups of butterflies, especially Tiger Swallowtails, huddled on the road. Chances are they are sitting on a pile of wolf dung, probing it for important salts and moisture. If you find wolf scats, be sure to stop and howl, and if possible, return at night to try again.

LEFT ABOVE: Only minutes after being subdued, the wolf regains consciousness.

LEFT BELOW: The fully revived wolf, now collared for life, is not long in heading for cover.

RIGHT: The transmitter allows researchers to follow the wolf for as long as the battery or the wolf remains alive. Due to the transmitter's mortality mode, a collared wolf can be located even after it has died.

In Wolf Country

If you expect to encounter a wolf every time you are out in the Algonquin wilds, most times you will be greatly disappointed. But if you consider a wolf encounter only as a bonus and view just being out there as the prime reward, then you will always leave fulfilled. There are countless other creatures, all as captivating as wolves. Even the smallest and most obscure can provide compelling insight into the complexity, drama, and even humor of the natural world.

It was mid-May and I was searching for wolf sign in an abandoned gravel pit not far from Lake Travers, my favourite lake in Algonquin. The day was relatively warm but mercifully the first biting flies of the season were not yet out. As I examined some old wolf paw prints in the soft mud, I heard a chorus of toad song coming from a shallow pond at the far end of the pit.

Remembering that I had no photographs of singing toads, I decided to abandon temporarily my search for wolves. I swapped my telephoto for a macro lens, donned my boots, and headed for the pond:

The piercing din suggests that at least a hundred male toads are calling for mates. Despite my efforts to wade slowly with as little disturbance as possible, the toads nearest me quickly fall silent. As I move towards the back part of the pond where other singers are still going strong, they, too, quickly develop laryngitis.

I decide my best option is to stand in one spot and wait. Sure enough, only a couple of minutes pass before the most distant

Each excursion into wolf country brings new adventures. This May day it was the sex lives of toads that enjoyably distracted me from the search for wolves.

▲ No matter how fleeting, every encounter with wolves
leaves us with more than a lasting memory.

toads start to call again. One by one, like an orchestra commencing a performance, from all across the pond others join in. After about 10 minutes the toads nearest me begin to sing.

It is fascinating to watch their throats swell up like little balloons. Through the camera lens I watch the toads close their tiny nostrils just before they force the air into these inflated resonating chambers. During a singing episode, the throat sacs vibrate rapidly, creating bands of ripples around the toads. While the males are highly visible, the Amazonian females are much harder to find, their much larger bodies floating just beneath the water surface. Their bulging eyes are about all that is visible as they attentively analyze the shrill promises trilled by their suitors.

Every now and again a competitor encroaches on another male's turf and a good old-fashioned donnybrook breaks out. Usually it is the intruder that is convinced to depart for calmer waters. Sometimes the victor returns to his post; other times he remains and sings his victory song from the battleground.

From reading up on the sex lives of frogs, I was aware that in some species, there are males that do not call. These non-singers hang around the edge of a serenader's territory and intercept the females that swim in to take a closer look at the performer. I soon observed that there are "satellite" males in the world of toads. It was great fun to see these silent sneakers in action, ambushing love-struck females on the move to a front-row seat. Perhaps hoping that she might mistake him for a singer, a satellite male would try his best to grasp an incoming female in a nuptial hug, known as amplexus. The females I saw thus mugged were not fooled and quickly tossed aside the pests like last week's news. The conniving toads were obviously not selective, for males that were off to do battle were also considered fair game for their advances. Whenever the wrong choice was made, the satellite male was not long in learning the error of his ways.

After an embarrassing number of rolls of film had been shot, my back told me it was time to go. When I returned to my truck I learned that I had been in the pond no less than four and a half hours. Yet during that time I never once considered going back to search for wolves. Much later, having failed to turn up any fresh wolf sign after leaving the pond, I returned home, yet was not disappointed with the day. I had witnessed a most fascinating spectacle, in a place where wild wolves roam. It had been a special day.

As long as you keep your ears and eyes open, you will never come back without a "trophy." Every excursion will yield a wealth of treasured memories. For me, it is not so much a potential encounter with wolves and other wild creatures that keeps me returning to the wilds as it is the experience of being totally immersed in nature. Also, each trip into wolf country is in part an introspective journey. As I sit alone on a forest slope or slice my paddle through gentle waters, away from all the unnatural distractions that clutter our lives, I find the time to reflect on life's important issues.

Wolves are quintessential components of the wilderness psyche, and our search for them is as much a spiritual adventure as it is a physical endeavour. No matter how fleeting the encounter, any meeting with a wolf leaves us with much more than a lasting memory. When we walk where their paws have tread, we enter a world from our past. When we hear their howls, we hear the heartbeat of the wilderness. And when we look into a wolf's eyes, we see the unfettered spirit of all that is wild.

ABOUT THE PHOTOGRAPHS

Unlike the captive "model" wolves that appear in most books and magazines, the animals in this book are wild, free-ranging wolves. Algonquin wolves are elusive and extremely difficult to see, let alone photograph. Extensive planning, effort, and a certain amount of luck went into the making of each photograph in this book. Unless you are fully prepared to expend the time and energy, you should really not plan on photographing wolves during an Algonquin visit.

I urge you to avoid approaching dens or rendezvous sites. Wolves are easily disturbed and might be forced to relocate if these sites are paid a visit. In the 25 years I have roamed Algonquin, I have visited rendezvous sites little more than a dozen times. Each visit involved hours of preparation.

Whenever I am looking for or photographing wolves (or anything else, for that matter), if there is any likelihood that my efforts will scare off the animals, I abandon the endeavour. It is important to intrude as little as possible into the lives of all wild things. Also, it is ethically and morally wrong to disturb wolves or any other wild creature in order to get a photograph. The subject is always more important than the potential picture. Oddly enough, the more respect I show for wild things, the more photographic opportunities I seem to receive.

However, respect alone will not get you photographs. It is also important to have proper equipment, quality film, a sturdy tripod, good technique, and an intimate knowledge of the subject matter. I use Canon camera equipment; an Eos 1N body fitted with a 500 f4.5L lens provides me with the sharpness of image and magnification necessary to photograph wolves. A Swiss Arc Ball Head mounted on a Gitzo tripod gives smoothness of movement and overall stability.

I prefer Kodak film over most other brands, and Kodachrome 25 ASA is undeniably my favourite. Its sharpness, fine grain structure, and excellent rendition of brown and grey tones make it perfect for properly recording the subtle colours of wolves. But the obvious drawback is its speed. Since wolf encounters often take place at dawn or dusk, when light is at a premium, a faster-speed film has advantages at these times of day. Kodak recently came out with a new high-speed film that resolves this problem quite nicely. The Kodak 100 SW professional slide film is surprisingly sharp and has excellent colour, including the browns and greens that other films tend to find problematic. In the dim light associated with early morning and evening shooting, this film (along with my fast 500 lens) enables me to use the shutter speed I need for wolf photography. Some of the photographs at rendezvous sites were taken with this film and at a camera shutter speed of one-eighth of a second or less.

A deep knowledge of the subject matter is critical to getting a good shot. The books and references listed in "Further Reading" will certainly help you expand your knowledge of wolves. If you are coming to Algonquin Park, the excellent bookstore located in the Visitor Centre has many of the recommended titles.

FURTHER READING

The following brief list of books and publications will enhance your knowledge, and therefore your enjoyment, of wolves.

GENERAL BIOLOGY

Dekker, Dick. *Wolf Story*. Edmonton: BST Publications, 1994.

Mech, David L. *The Wolf*. Garden City, NY: The Natural History Press, 1970.

Murray, John A (ed.). *Out Among the Wolves: Contemporary Writings on the Wolf*. Vancouver: Whitecap Books, 1993.

Rutter, R.J., and D.H. Pimlott. *The World of the Wolf*. New York, NY: J.B. Lippincott Company, 1968.

HOWLING

Strickland, Dan. *Wolf Howling in Algonquin Provincial Park*. Algonquin Technical Bulletin No. 3. The Friends of Algonquin Park, 1988.

RESEARCH

Lawrence, R.D. *In Praise of Wolves*. Toronto: Collins
Publishers, 1986.

Pimlott, D.H., Shannon, J.A., and G.B. Kolenosky. *The
Ecology of the Timber Wolf in Algonquin Provincial Park*.
Department of Lands and Forests Research Branch
Research Report (Wildlife) No. 7, 1969.

Theberge, John and Mary. *Adventures with Algonquin Wolves*.
Faculty of Environmental Studies, University of
Waterloo, 1993.

Theberge, John and Mary. *Wolves and Wolf Research in
Algonquin Park*. Faculty of Environmental Studies,
University of Waterloo, 1990.

Theberge, John. *Wolves and Wilderness*. Toronto: Dent
Canada, 1975.